I0092668

THE
RELATIONSHIP
BETWEEN
STRATEGIC
SUCCESS
PARADIGM AND
PERFORMANCE IN
NONPROFIT
HOSPITALS

DR. ROBERT C. MEYERS, DBA, MSA, BS

Copyright © 2023 by Dr. Robert C. Meyers, DBA, MSA, BS

Paperback: 978-1-963050-26-4
eBook: 978-1-963050-23-3
Hardback: 978-1-963050-22-6
Library of Congress Control Number: 2023922457

All rights reserved. No part of this publication may be reproduced, distributed, or transmitted in any form or by any electronic or mechanical means, without the prior written permission of the publisher, except in the case of brief quotations embodied in critical reviews and certain other noncommercial uses permitted by copyright law.

This Book is a work of Nonfiction.

Ordering Information:

Prime Seven Media
518 Landmann St.
Tomah City, WI 54660

Printed in the United States of America

Acknowledgements

I would like to express my deepest appreciation to family, friends, and mentors for inspiring me to complete my book. They motivated and encouraged me throughout the process to finish my book. Also, thank you to my publishing company for their contributions in assisting me to complete and publish my book. A special thanks to Dr. Yousef Ibrahim and other mentors for constantly inspiring and guiding me.

Abstract

THE PROBLEM: There is no empirical research that relates nonprofit hospital's performance with the strategic success paradigm factors of strategic aggressiveness, capability responsiveness, environmental turbulence, and legitimacy in nonprofit hospitals. The study is to determine, if there is a relationship among the components of the strategic success paradigm and performance in nonprofit hospitals. The study attempts to close the gap between the strategic success hypothesis (Environmental turbulence, strategic aggressiveness, and capability responsiveness), and other strategic management variables with performance measures of Joint Commission Accreditation, Hospital Consumer Assessment of Healthcare Providers & Systems (HCAHPS), and financial performance in nonprofit hospitals.

METHOD: A descriptive / correlational study of nonprofit hospitals' strategic success factors (environmental turbulence, strategic aggressiveness, capability responsiveness), strategic posture, and legitimacy and their performance (financial performance, Joint Commission Accreditation, and Hospital Consumer Assessment of Healthcare Providers & Systems).

The target population for this research included nonprofit hospitals or health systems in the United States that participated in Joint Commission Accreditation for Hospitals and Hospital Consumer Assessment of Healthcare Providers & Systems (HCAHPS). An online survey was used to collect responses from 43 nonprofit hospitals and health systems for a correlational study. The study investigated different aspects of the Strategic Success paradigm developed by Ansoff (1984) and examined the relationship among the nonprofit hospitals' environmental turbulence, strategy aggressiveness, capability responsiveness, strategic posture and legitimacy. The two intervening variables, defined as the gaps measured the absolute and actual difference between strategic aggressiveness and environmental turbulence and capability responsiveness and environmental turbulence and the financial and quality of care performance measures of nonprofit hospitals in the United States. Hospitals are faced with increasing pressure to improve performance and quality of care while reducing costs. The existing literature does not address strategic success factors on hospital performance and efficiency. In this Book, I utilized the components of Dr. Ansoff's strategic success factors to analyze the performance of federal, state, and local nonprofit hospitals in the United States. The study includes an introduction to the statement of the problem; the research problem and purpose of the study. Also, it provides the general theoretical framework of the study, a literature review, the research methodology of the study, the research findings, and a summary & conclusions.

The main objective of the study was to examine nonprofit hospitals utilizing Dr. Ansoff's strategic success factors with both qualitative and quantitative data to validate the effects of Dr. Ansoff's strategic success paradigms. Currently, hospitals use a variety of different measurement tools. These include the Joint Commission on Accreditation of Healthcare Organizations Criteria (JCAHO), Hospital Consumer Assessment of Healthcare Organizations, financial measures, Lean six sigma criteria, balanced scorecard, Healthcare Effectiveness Data and Information Set (HEDIS), and other quality metrics.

RESULTS: Seven hypotheses were tested using Spearman's rho, a non-parametric measure of statistical dependence between 2 variables with a significance level of 5% ($p < .05$). Two hypotheses (1, 4) tested the relationship between financial performance and strategic aggressiveness gap and strategic aggressiveness and found no significance between nonprofit hospitals' financial performance, strategic aggressiveness or the gap; hence they were not supported. Hypotheses 2 tested the relationship between the quality of care performance measures: Joint Commission Accreditation and Hospital Consumer Assessment of Healthcare Providers & Systems (HCAHPS) and capability responsiveness gap, was supported ($[r] = .322$, $p = .038$; $[r] = .352$, $p = .022$).

Hypothesis 3, tested the relationship between the nonprofit hospitals' capability responsiveness and quality performance measures of Joint Commission Accreditation and Hospital Consumer Assessment of Healthcare Providers & Systems

(HCAHPS), was supported ([r] = .322, p = .038); [r] = .395, p = .022). Hypothesis 5, relating nonprofit hospitals' strategic posture and quality of care performance measures of Joint Commission Accreditation and Hospital Consumer Assessment of Healthcare Providers & Systems was supported ([r] = .321, p = .038). Hypothesis 6, relating to nonprofit hospitals' legitimacy and quality of care performance measures: Joint Commission Accreditation and Hospital Consumer Assessment of Healthcare Providers & Systems was supported ([r] = .375, p = .013). Hypothesis 7, the relationship between environmental turbulence and strategic posture was supported ([r] = -.459, p = .002).

Table of Contents

List of Tables

List of Figures

CHAPTER 1

Background of
the Problem

*D*uring the past 20 to 30 years, the healthcare industry has changed dramatically and has taken on a whole new role in society. There have been countless improvements in modern medicine, and with the rapid changes in technology, public policy, and patient needs, healthcare costs will continue to grow. We can compare healthcare costs today to those of 20 years ago as one way of illuminating the evolutionary changes in the United States healthcare system. We can go back to the end of 1999, when healthcare costs were over $1.07 trillion and accounted for only 14% of the U.S. Gross Domestic Product (GDP). By the end of 2008, expenditures on healthcare in the United States had surpassed $2.3 trillion—more than twice the cost in 1999—and accounted for 16.2% of the nation's GDP. In 2016, healthcare costs rose to more than $3.6 trillion and accounted for over 18% of the nation's GDP (Munro, 2016). This is among the highest healthcare cost in all industrialized countries. Although the federal government and Former President Obama passed a healthcare reform bill, healthcare costs continue to rise and the overall economic slowdown and rising federal deficit are placing great strains on the system. Some of the major contributing factors to rising healthcare costs are new technology, prescription drugs, an aging population, and increasing hospital costs. The nation's efforts to control healthcare costs have not had much of a long-term effect, prompting a debate over whether such proposals are able to sustainably reduce costs and improve quality outcomes.

Statement of the Problem

Hospital costs have continued to be the highest percentage of healthcare costs, accounting for more than 32% of all healthcare costs, or over $800 billion in 2012 and over $1.3 Trillion in 2021 NHE Fact Sheet 2021 https://www.cms.gov/data-research/statistics-trends-and-reports/national-health-expenditure-data/nhe-fact-sheet). The past economic recession, changing healthcare policies, increased public scrutiny of healthcare services and demand for quality has caused hospitals and other healthcare organizations to become more efficient. Today, hospitals are investing in newer technology, adjusting provider compensation, increasing preventive care, and increasing consumer involvement. There is a need for more empirical research related to effective strategic success hypotheses and performance in the healthcare industry. Also, there is a need to establish standardized quality and performance measurements for determining the success of federal, state and local nonprofit hospitals. Healthcare organizations will continue to need more effective strategic planning methods well into the future.

This study will utilize the components of Dr. Ansoff's strategic success factors to analyze the performance of nonprofit hospitals. The study will determine if the strategic success factors could be an effective measurement tool to analyze hospitals' performance effectiveness. Currently, hospitals use a variety of different measurement tools.

These include the Joint Commission on Accreditation of Healthcare Organizations Criteria, Lean Six Sigma criteria, Healthcare Effectiveness Data and Information Set (HEDIS), Balanced scorecard, and other quality metrics. All these are used to determine hospitals' performance effectiveness. Although these criteria measure a hospital's performance and management effectiveness, they do not provide a concrete foundation or roadmap for how strategic success can be achieved by nonprofit hospitals. Little is known about the impact of environmental factors on nonprofit hospitals, or how these hospitals respond to changes in the environment and other factors. The healthcare industry has undergone tremendous changes over the past few decades, and nonprofit hospitals have been severely impacted.

Research Problem

Nonprofit hospitals have closed their doors or merged with other larger hospital systems due to poor performance, lack of efficiency, and inadequate quality of care (Harrison, McCue, Wang 2003). Across the country, state and local nonprofit hospitals have struggled to provide a return on investment and provide efficient quality healthcare to the community (Cutler, 2000). Though progress has been made, the nation is still struggling to determine the soundest and most reliable metrics to gauge the effectiveness and efficiency of processes and outcomes of nonprofit hospitals (Finlayson et al. 2002; Clarke and Oakley 2007).

Additionally, finding a way to properly measure quality and cost of healthcare continues to be a problem. Such challenges have been especially prominent in performance reporting and appraisals of quality (Leonardi, McGory, and Ko 2007). Nevertheless, performance reports are still widely disseminated, especially with the American public. There is a need for better performance, more efficiency, and higher quality in the hospital industry.

This chapter presents the background of the research problem, a statement of the problem, and a discussion of the importance of this research to the field of strategic management and the hospital industry. Nonprofit hospitals provide healthcare services to a variety of patients, but quality and efficiency has lagged behind for-profit hospitals for decades (Ransom, Joshi, Nash, Ransom, 2008). There have been numerous criteria used to measure the performance, quality, and efficiency of hospitals, but very few have attempted to evaluate the performance, quality, and efficiency of nonprofit hospitals across the spectrum of nonprofit hospitals.

Little is known about the impact of environmental factors on the success of nonprofit hospitals, or how nonprofit hospitals respond to changes in their environment. This study attempts to establish relationships among the components of the strategic success factors and performance in nonprofit hospitals. The study attempts to close the gap between the strategic success factors (environmental turbulence, strategic aggressiveness of the organization, and capability responsiveness) affecting performance in nonprofit hospitals. Also, the study attempts to establish a direct correlation between the nonprofit hospital strategy, legitimacy and how it affects performance in nonprofit hospitals. In addition, the study attempts to develop a basis for further research on the topic. The study is focused on the strategic success paradigm and performance of nonprofit hospitals.

Purpose of the Study

The purpose of this study is to establish a relationship among the components of Dr. Ansoff's Strategic Success paradigm, organizational strategies, and performance in federal, state, and local nonprofit hospitals.

The study hopes to determine whether the Strategic Success Model could be used to improve the overall performance of nonprofit hospitals. Also, I hope to provide a correlation between the strategic success paradigm for nonprofit hospitals, healthcare organizations and their overall performance effectiveness. The study attempts to close the gap between the Strategic Success Model (environmental turbulence, strategic aggressiveness, and capability responsiveness) and issues affecting performance in nonprofit hospitals.

In addition, it hopes to provide a correlation between hospital strategy and performance. Also, the study hopes to use Ansoff's Strategic Success Model from 1965 to determine, if it's still relevant in today turbulent healthcare industry.

Dr. Ansoff's insight came from the works of Emery and Trist (1965), which described the external environment as being composed of several distinctive segments at different levels of turbulence. Although, it has been proven in several industries that an organization's performance is optimal when its strategic behavior and capability match the turbulence of the environment, but it has not been proven in the nonprofit hospital industry. I hope to prove that a hospital's or healthcare organization's performance is optimized when its strategic behavior and capability responsiveness are aligned to match its environment. In addition, I want to show the connection between nonprofit hospitals' performance and competitive/ organizational strategies.

Contribution to the Academic Field of Strategic Management

The contribution of this study to the academic field of strategic management will be to develop a framework representing an emerging theoretical perspective showing a relationship between Ansoff's Strategic Success Paradigm and overall performance in the hospital industry.

Also, I was able to bridge the gap between nonprofit federal, state, and local hospitals' performance effectiveness and the use of strategic management tools. Another contribution of this study to the academic field of strategic and healthcare management will be to demonstrate the connection between Dr. Ansoff's strategic success factors and the performance effectiveness of nonprofit hospitals. This researcher hopes to discover the connections that can help fill the gap between nonprofit hospitals' performance and the most effective performance each organization can attain.

Contribution to the Practice of Strategic Management

Hospital administrators, CEOs, and directors face difficult challenges because the hospital and healthcare industry are in an increasingly turbulent environment. The contribution of this study to the practice of strategic management will be to show the connection between Ansoff's strategic success factors and hospital strategic management. Some of the driving forces that determine the success of a hospital's strategic behavior are the turbulence in the external environment, the hospital's strategic aggressiveness, and its capability responsiveness. In addition, other factors shaping the performance of hospitals are their competitive/organizational strategies and the legitimacy in the healthcare industry.

This researcher sought to improve on the contingent theory developed by Ansoff (1976) and the work of Emery and Trist

(1965) by going a step further to validate their theories on the performance of nonprofit federal, state, and local hospitals and healthcare organizations. There have been many books that have further validated the strategic success model, but few have validated the strategic success model in the nonprofit hospital/healthcare organization industry. This book hopes to validate the strategic success model in the nonprofit hospital/healthcare industry.

This research may assist nonprofit hospital leaders by supporting the theory that a nonprofit hospital's environmental turbulence, responsiveness capabilities and their strategic aggressiveness does support improved performance outcomes. Chapter two of this study presents a review of relevant literature on strategic planning in nonprofit hospitals, environment turbulence in the healthcare industry, capability responsiveness of nonprofit hospitals. Also, chapter two presents literature on aggressiveness of nonprofit hospitals strategic behavior, and the importance of hospital's mission, vision and goals. It goes on to discuss the forces/trends in the hospital industry, nonprofit hospital strategies, and strategic posture/intent.

Chapter 2B presents the research model, variables, performance measures, research questions & hypotheses, and the conceptual & operational definitions. Chapter three presents the research methodology and details of the research design, measures, research procedures, variables, and analytical procedures utilized. Chapter four applies the obtained data and research findings, statistical analysis and specified analytical and statistical tests. Chapter five includes the summary, expected contributions of the study, theoretical framework and discussion of the findings and recommendations for future research, methodology and details of the research design.

General Theoretical Framework

*T*his chapter will present the broad context of relationships affecting nonprofit federal, state and local hospitals and healthcare organizations. The major theoretical concepts and the basis upon which this study was formed are presented in two parts. The first part, Chapter 2A, presents the global model, which provides a descriptive model of the relationships between the hospital/healthcare organization industry's internal and external environmental factors and Ansoff's strategic success hypothesis for nonprofit hospitals. Also, it illustrates the connection between the hospital/healthcare organization industry's internal and external factors and performance.

The objective of this chapter is to create a general framework for analyzing the environment of nonprofit federal, state, and local hospitals and the internal and external factors affecting their performance outcomes and operations. There is little published analytical work on the relationship between strategic behavior and performance outcomes in nonprofit hospitals/ healthcare organizations.

This study will provide a comprehensive description of strategic behavior in hospitals/healthcare organizations and their performance. This chapter introduces the research questions, hypotheses, and operational and conceptual definitions of the variables.

The global model is divided into three sections: (a) a description of the global model, (b) a literature review that supports the global model, and (c) a discussion of the global model sections.

Description of the Global Model

The global model depicted in Figure 1 presents the comprehensive organizational factors affecting nonprofit hospitals. Figure 1 shows the strategic and operating behavior of hospitals/healthcare organizations. The left side of the global model shows the internal environmental factors and their relationship to hospital/healthcare organizations performance. The right side depicts the external environment and its relationship to hospital/healthcare organizations performance. Also, the global model covers Ansoff's strategic success factors and their relationship to hospital/healthcare organization performance.

Both left and right sides of the global model represent the global forces impacting hospitals' performance outcomes and operation. It is a theoretical framework for evaluating the effectiveness of strategic management in healthcare and the challenges facing nonprofit hospitals/healthcare organizations.

GLOBAL MODEL

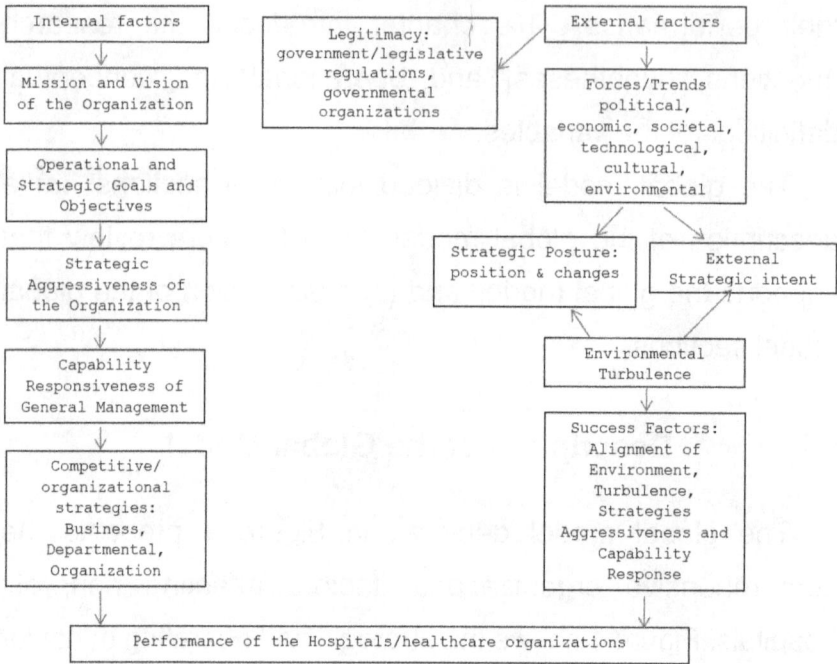

Figure 1. Global model of strategic behavior in Hospitals

Literature Review That Supports the Global Model

The literature review section breaks down the hospital/ healthcare organization industry's internal and external environment, and Ansoff's Strategic Success Model. The literature illustrates the relationship between the internal and external environment of nonprofit hospitals/healthcare organizations and Dr. Ansoff's Strategic Success Model. Also, it describes the connection between the hospital industry's internal and external environment and Dr. Ansoff's Strategic Success Paradigm in relation to hospital/healthcare organization performance outcomes. Nonprofit hospitals are based on their charitable purpose and sometimes affiliated with a religious denomination. Nonprofit hospitals/healthcare organizations are distinct from private for-profit hospitals. Nonprofit hospitals/ healthcare organizations focus is on improving quality, efficiency and increasing market share (Rodak, 2012). In 2016, there were a little more than 2,845 nonprofit community hospitals; 983 state and local government community hospitals; 212 federal nonprofit hospitals, and 401 nonfederal Psychiatric hospitals (NHE Fast Fact, 2016). In 2016, total hospital spending increased by 5.6% to $1.036 trillion faster than the 4.6% growth in 2016 nonprofit community hospital expenses totaled an estimated $1.07 trillion (NHE Fact Sheet 2017).

Strategic Planning in Hospitals

Healthcare organizations have used strategic planning sporadically since the 1970s, orienting it toward providing services and meeting the needs of the population.

Despite the uncertainties about its value, strategic planning is being used frequently and is considered critical to the success of healthcare organizations (Zuckerman, 2012). Strategic planning in hospitals is now a discipline that has been embraced only recently by hospital administrators (Luke, Walston, & Plummer, 2004).

It's no longer a thing of the past but has evolved into a strategic process that Hospital Administrators and Governing boards are consistently reviewing (Greene, 2009). In order to meet goals of improved quality and reduce costs in today's changing healthcare environment, hospitals are being forced to be creative and flexible in their strategies (Rodak, 2012). Formal strategic planning requires a sizable investment of organizational time and other resources, and strategic planning is commonly believed to be important to the effective functioning of healthcare organizations. However, evidence on the practice of strategic planning is scarce (Kaissi, et., 2008). Leaders generally support the perspective that strategic planning is a key component of their role as strategic managers. This is based on the belief that organizations guided by correct strategies perform better and that organizational leaders make better strategic choices if they were able to more accurately read their internal and external environments (Luke, Walston, and Plummer 2004). The benefits of strategic planning include the creation of organizational focus, mobilization of stakeholders, and motivation of the workforce, in addition to the development of better strategies (Begun and Heatwole, 1999). Hospitals and health systems continue to consolidate and purchase physician practices.

The value of strategic planning in an environment characterized by increased uncertainty and greater & faster change continues to be the most pressing and immediate concerns for nonprofit hospitals. Leading healthcare organizations are recognizing that strategic planning and the focus and prioritization that it calls for is more important now than ever before.

With increasingly scarce resources, larger, more diverse and geographically dispersed organizations and uncertainty in a fast-paced environment, strategic planning is being adapted to be more relevant to contemporary organizations. Healthcare leaders are advancing strategic planning from a periodic exercise to a more continuous and integrated strategic management process (Zuckerman, 2014). While historically strategic planning in healthcare has focused nearly exclusively on growth through increasing market share and expanding the market, strategic planning today includes five new imperatives: Sufficient scale and scope or niche play; cost competitiveness; demonstrated quality; exceptional service and real integration. Strategic planning or better yet, strategic management is an increasingly important discipline in today's rapidly changing healthcare environment. Strategic management allows leaders to exert better control or influence over these external forces and steer their organizations toward a new future (2014).

Hospital administrators had to assume greater responsibility for planning and budgeting to respond to the growing complexities of medicine (Shi, Singh, 2008). The evolution of the hospital administrator to hospital chief executive officer (CEO) reflected a transition in hospital administration according to Beckham (2000, p. 57). Hospitals and healthcare organizations operate in a competitive environment, and CEO's attempt to position their organizations to be high performing and efficient

(Luke et al., 2004). Clearly, successful organizations adapt to their environments to survive and prosper. Nonprofit hospitals are complicated entities designed not only to provide healthcare services, but also to play key roles in health-related research and education. As well show important general economic developmental roles in their communities (Longest, 2010).

One of the key areas of focus for hospitals is their strategic planning/management abilities. Scholars define strategic planning as moving from a point in the present to some point in the future in the face of an environment of uncertainty and resistance (Beckham, 2000; Kaleba, 2006). Uncertainty and resistance to organizational change often emanate from within a hospital as physicians, staff, patients, and stakeholders emerge as distinct and powerful internal organizational forces. All nonprofit hospitals affected by circumstances in their external environments and making successful strategic decisions requires that they have researched and analyzed all external factors (Glass, Zell, & Duron, 2005).

Some of the vital component of a hospital's internal factors is their mission, vision, and values statement and whether its structure and processes allow it to achieve its purpose and business aims. The structure of governance and management are evaluated considering the mission, vision, and values in comparison to similar organizations review of effectiveness and efficiency (Zuckerman, 2012). Physicians are an influential internal force within a hospital because it is important for them to participate in the design and development of a hospital's strategic plan (Kelly, 2008). Another powerful internal influence comes from staff (nurses, administrative staff, and technicians) because satisfied employees effectively participate in the operations of an organization and can be an organization's most valuable asset (Bassi & McMurrer, 2007). Utilized ineffectively, employees are the source of poor organizational performance and can contribute to organizational failure. A third internal influencer is patients because they affect the behaviors and work environment of physicians and staff. The fourth internal factor is the board of trustees.

While board composition can affect strategic planning (Devers 2001), board behavior and power can dramatically and directly influence the overall performance of a hospital/healthcare organization and the administrative staff's work environment (Alexander, Fennell, & Halpern 1993).

Recognizing and addressing these powerful internal influencing forces is fundamental to hospital/healthcare organizations strategic planning. External forces can create uncertainty and resistance in strategic planning as environmental challenges continue to influence organizational performance. In remarks to hospital CEOs, Thomas C. Dolan, Ph.D., FACHE, CAE, Former President and CEO of the American College of Healthcare Executives, stated, "Ten to twenty years ago, a trend in one part of the country might take years to get to your area." In today's, global economy, it can happen in a matter of months, and you need to be prepared (Zuckerman, 2012, p. 1). Some of the external forces impacting hospitals are innovative technology, changes in government regulations (i.e. Affordable Care Act, Medicare & Medicaid pay-for-performance system, Joint Commission Standards, etc..), Infectious disease outbreaks, competitors, and increased pressure from insurance companies for hospitals to improve quality of care and shift to value-based care (Kash, 2016).

Discussion of the Global Model

The global model depicted in Figure 1 shows the coexistence of strategic and operating behaviors. The left side of the global model shows the internal environmental factors, and the right side depicts the factors affecting the external environmental factors influencing the strategic behavior of hospitals and their operating behavior.

It describes the research problem and the associated research hypotheses, and the conceptual and operational definition of the variables for the purpose of the study. This study sought to apply principles of strategic management to the practice of hospital management.

It concludes with a brief discussion of a framework for evaluating the effectiveness of strategic management in hospitals and healthcare organizations. Literature was reviewed for both the general practice of strategic management in hospitals with applications to specific functional activities, as well as the more specialized area of hospital management. The primary framework under which this study was conducted is the Strategic Success Model developed by the late Dr. H.

Igor Ansoff. However, this study drew heavily on research conducted for hospital, Healthcare strategic management and the resource-based view of strategic management. Hospital/healthcare organization's strategies are postulated to follow an analogous process as the strategic management of an overall organization.

In the research model, changes in healthcare regulations and policy lead to the perception of healthcare turbulence, which is a measure of the healthcare costs in the United States that have been increasing for decades. Expenditures in the United States on healthcare surpassed $3.3 trillion in 2016, and were more than $2.3 trillion in 2008, more than three times the $714 billion spent in 1990. Medicare expenditures grew to over $672.1 billion and over $565 billion in 2016. Healthcare costs increased to over 19% of GDP in 2020, Average annual healthcare spending is projected to grow at an average of (5.6%) per year and anticipated to outpace average annual growth in the overall economy by about 2 percentage points (Martin, Lassman, Washington, & Catlin, 2012).

In 2020, national healthcare spending reached $4.3 trillion and comprise 19% of GDP. Enrollment growth, Medicaid coverage expansions, and exchange plan premium and cost-sharing subsidies increased cost.

The government-sponsored share of healthcare spending increased from 45% in 2010 to about 50% in 2021, driven by expected robust Affordable Care Act enrollment, Medicare, and Medicaid cost (NHE Fact Sheet 2021). Stemming this growth has become a major policy priority as government, employers, and consumers increasingly struggle to keep up with rising healthcare costs. In 2016, Under Former Republican President Trump, and a Republican controlled House and Senate, the affordable care act would be dismantled and over 24 million people would lose coverage over the next decade. The Congressional Budget Office estimated that the bill would spike premiums in individual insurance markets in 2018, 2019 and beyond by 15% to 20%, but rates would later start decreasing in 2020. This spike in individual insurance premiums would initially increase healthcare expenditure, but would later decrease costs (Meyer and Dickson, 2017). Some of the external forces affecting the hospital industry strategic planning are the changes to the Affordable Care Act (ACA), patient and insurance companies, CMS demand for increased quality and reduced cost. Other external forces affecting hospitals are partnerships with other healthcare organizations, increased competition, and implementation of newer medical electronic technology, rapidly aging population, and the development of community health programs. All hospitals are facing physicians, nurses, and healthcare staff shortages (Powers, Sanders, Stephens, 2013). These are only some of the external factors affecting the hospital industry in today's turbulent environment.

Environmental Turbulence in the Healthcare Industry

Environmental turbulence refers to the changeability, predictability, novelty of change, and complexity of the environment for hospitals. The two characteristics of changeability are the complexity and familiarity of events. For predictability, the characteristics are rapidity of change and visibility of the future. Level one of the five levels correspond with the least complexity and the fewest unknown factors in the environment. The speed of change is slow, events and changeability are familiar, and the future is based on the past. Level one in environmental turbulence is defined as repetitive and level five as unpredictable. Ansoff and McDonnell (1990) defined environmental turbulence as a combined measurement of changeability and predictability. Changeability reflects the complexity and relative novelty of changes in an organization's environment. Predictability measures the clarity and completeness of a firm's information at the time strategic decisions need to be made (Ansoff & McDonnell, 1990). Kim and Thompson (2012) theorized that Environmental munificence refers to the level of abundance of critical resources for an organization and reflects the extent to which the environment can support the provision of hospital services and activities. While environmental complexity refers to the number and types of organizations existing in a focal organization's environment. Thus, competition intensifies as the number of similar organizations in a market increases (Kim, Thompson, 2012). Senior management's perception of environmental turbulence is a key element in studying the healthcare industry. Healthcare is facing a turbulent environment because of numerous factors such as increased competition, changes in Medicare/Medicaid reimbursement, staff turnover, and increasing pressure to implement new healthcare technology. Over the past few decades, healthcare costs have increased more rapidly in the United States than any other industrialized nation.

While overall cost inflation has slowed somewhat in recent years, hospital-based charges associated with Medicaid and Medicare has continued to climb. Three factors that have been identified as the primary contributors to increasing costs in hospital-based care: (1) demographic changes resulting in an increase in the number of elderly patients;

(2) rising labor costs; and development and acquisition of new medical technology (Friedman, Corvallis, Goes, 2000). The inflated cost associated with adoption of new technologies have been attributed to increased competition among hospitals. The acquisition of newer technology can be one of the most critical decisions a hospital makes and can have dramatic effects on the organization. Given the turbulent changes in the healthcare and hospital industry in the United States, most experts believe that strategic decisions in hospitals are being made with a high degree of uncertainty. Thus, organizations are continuously engaged in an iterative process of adaptation to changes in their external environment to survive (Swayne, Duncan, & Ginter, 2009).

The multi-faceted strategic decision making in these organizations is heavily affected by their public policy environments as by their business, demographic, technological or other external environments (Longest, 2012). While the external environments of nonprofit, public hospitals have many important components, public policy aspects are critical. Public hospital's strategically-relevant external environment includes all circumstances outside its physical boundaries that can influence its performance.

Typical public hospitals' external environments are extraordinarily complicated and directly impacted by all the external environmental factors. Public hospitals must assess the public-policy-driven threats and opportunities facing their organizations.

Public policy environments begin with the way government approaches the health of their citizenries, but for most public hospitals their public policy environment is complicated, turbulent and inevitably unpredictable (Longest, 2012, pg. 212). Some aspect of turbulence and unpredictability of these environments are seen in the multitude of preferences and actions exhibited in efforts to reform healthcare in the United States. These efforts have shown how unpredictable the public policies affecting public, nonprofit hospitals can be and the turbulence in which, public policy is made. Other environmental factors are pressures for improved efficiency, increased patient satisfaction, decrease in costs, and improved technology in the delivery of healthcare. One-way nonprofit hospitals are improving efficiency is through mergers and acquisitions.

Hospitals are being forced to consolidate for four important reasons. First, under value-based-purchasing payment systems and regulations, hospitals may face Medicare reimbursement cuts, if they are unable to meet quality and technological standards, such as meaningful use of an electronic health record. Second, large hospitals are absorbing smaller hospitals and physician practices to gain market share and control costs (Creswell & Abelson, 2013). Third is to encourage greater collaboration among healthcare providers with the intent of reducing costs, increasing efficiency, and improving care coordination. Finally, hospitals that provide a disproportionate share of care to the uninsured will begin to see federal subsidies dissipate on the premise that expanded Medicaid programs will make subsidies less necessary (Noles, Reiter, Pink, 2015).

Another major cause of environmental turbulence in hospitals is technical turbulence and the introduction of new medical and information technology as a factor in the competitive and environmental dynamics of the hospital industry (Devers, Brewster, Casalino 2003).

Technological turbulence can be based on the clinical IT configuration of the hospital and others in their environment. Hospitals are striving to improve their competitive position by being more market driven in their environment. Some nonprofit hospitals fit between levels two or three of the environmental turbulence scale, if they have been providing the same services in the same community for the entire period, they have been operating. As the turbulence level increases, there is more complexity and less predictability. Teaching hospitals are facing similar issues with highly unpredictable and an uncertain future. The high-level of turbulence threatens the financial viability of all hospitals, but especially the teaching hospitals, who haven't been exposed to a competitive environment before.

Hospitals are finding that in a competitive and turbulent market there is very little distinction between for-profit and not-for-profit hospitals, private and public, or teaching and community hospitals. The fundamental issue is economic survival. All hospitals must focus on their competitive strategy to remain viable. In a 1998 study used by academic medical centers showed that the overall degree of turbulence was high among all teaching hospital markets (Langabeer, 1998).

Based on research the environmental turbulence in hospitals can include both their external and internal environmental factors. Their external environment includes stakeholders, innovative technologies, competitors (managed care organizations), government and regulatory agencies, and public policy. Their internal environment includes the hospital's mission, vision, goals, values, organizational climate and culture, and the impact of regulations.

The internal environment is affected by the external environment, and with the major changes in healthcare, environmental turbulence has accelerated. When the internal environment is either ignored or marginalized, threats to morale, trust, quality, and economic success are created (Freed, 2005).

These changes are characterized by an intense demand for cost reduction, costly technological advances, and increased demand for quality services, along with strict government regulations and shifting consumer expectations. In this rapidly changing and increasingly constrained environment, providers that learn how to lower their costs in a sustainable manner while maintaining or improving outcomes can survive and prosper (Porter, 2010; Porter, Pabo, & Lee, 2013). We point to recently passed historic legislation on healthcare reform in the United States, as well as to several critical trends underlying the healthcare sector: (a) the need for a delivery system that can some-how address diverse problems as chronic diseases, aging, and bioterrorism; (b) trends in biotechnology, information technology, and personalized medicine; and (c) continued disparities in access to various levels of care and to high quality care. The evidence shows that the environments of health-care organizations have continued to evolve in even more complex and turbulent ways (Fennell, Adams, 2011). In today's society, one of the major issues facing healthcare organizations is cost reduction. Costs have become the focus of federal, state and local healthcare policies because government is the major payer of healthcare costs for nonprofit hospitals and healthcare organizations. The implementation of the Affordable Care Act (ACA) helped reduce costs and increase quality of care, but at what cost to the patients? (Bennett, A. R. 2012). From 2011 through 2013, the growth in hospital spending accelerated, reaching 5.3% in 2013 and 7.2% in 2014.

This faster growth rate reflects increases in service use due to the coverage expansions under the Affordable Care Act, Medicaid, and private insurance, partially offset by lower Medicare payment rate increases for hospitals mandated by the Affordable Care Act. Hospital spending grew to over 5% per year during the period of 2015–2020 with Medicare spending growth generally outpacing private health insurance spending growth, reflecting the shift of baby boomers onto Medicare. Medicare spending grew to over 8% in 2021. The future of nonprofit hospitals/healthcare organizations are affected by the government and business sectors. New governmental policies and regulations play a key role in the environment of hospitals because of their impact on costs and technological advances. Former President Obama's Healthcare Reform Law (Affordable Care Act) had increased government spending in healthcare by billions of dollars by expanding medical coverage to millions of uninsured or underinsured people. Nonprofit hospitals/ healthcare organizations have seen an increase in the number of patients they are treating and less money from Medicare and Medicaid. Medicare and Medicaid programs account for more than half the revenue in most of the nation's almost 3,000 community, nonprofit hospitals, including almost 1,000 Public hospitals controlled by state and local governments (National Health Expenditure Projections, 2016). The Centers for Medicare and Medicaid Services (CMS) changed the way hospitals interact with patients when it implemented a pay-for-performance (P4P) system. The program seeks to reward healthcare providers, who expand their focus from solely delivering a highly technical set of services that improved the patient's health to creating an atmosphere that makes hospitalization more humane and respectful of patients' values and preferences.

Globally, public and private payers seek to improve healthcare quality and lower costs through value-based purchasing (VBP) programs, which is a pay-for-performance system (Addink, Bankart, Murtagh, Baker, 2011; Sakai, 2012; Boucher, 2012; Pearson, 2012). Public policy is another area of environmental turbulence causing uncertainty in nonprofit hospitals as administrators and managers must constantly analyze and assess the impact of their public policy on their environment (Longest, 2010, p.216).

Nonprofit hospital expenditures are expected to rise dramatically over the next several years based on the number of people with healthcare insurance. Factors that hospitals are concerned about dramatically decrease the number of people and families with healthcare insurance. Also, the global pandemic strained many hospital financial resources and dramatically increased labor cost (Whaley, Demirkan, Bai, 2023).

Strategic Aggressiveness in the Healthcare Industry

The underlying premise of this research is based on Ansoff and McDonnell's (1990) Strategic Success Paradigm. When an organization matches its strategic aggressiveness and the responsiveness of its capability with its environmental turbulence, the organization has the greatest potential for future success (1990). Strategic aggressiveness is described in terms of the degree of discontinuity from the past of the organization's new services, competitive environments, and marketing strategies and timeliness of the introduction of the organization's new products/services relative to new products/services which have appeared on the market (Ansoff, McDonnell, 1990).

Hospital strategic aggressiveness is an important part of the hospital's overall strategy to reduce cost and improve quality (McLaughlin, Militello, 2015). The more involved senior management is in strategy implementation, new healthcare service development and marketing, the better their response to their environment. Hospital strategic aggressiveness focuses on the hospital's implementation of new services, healthcare marketing, management strategy, implementation of new healthcare technology, and their competitive environment. As turbulence increases, it becomes increasingly important for healthcare organizations to formulate and execute effective strategies that can provide a competitive advantage over other healthcare organizations (Langabeer, 1998).

In today's rapidly changing healthcare environment, hospitals and healthcare organizations are developing ways to reduce costs while maintaining or improving patient outcomes and expanding services. Nonprofit hospitals face serious financial challenges in the current healthcare environment and in response are altering their service offerings, by eliminating services that loses money and adding new services where profitability is expected to be greater (Kirby, Spetz, Maiuro, Scheffler, 2006). Some of the new services hospitals have been adding are inpatient rehabilitation centers, dialysis, and cardiology surgical services. In addition, genetic analysis and advanced diagnostic test are other new services hospitals are offering their patients (O'Brien, Kaluzny, Sheps, 2014). As part of the transformation to value-based care, many hospitals are focusing on innovative technology and strategies in population health, which are the core goals of healthcare reform (Rodak, 2012).

Hospital leadership is setting objectives to increase the value and quality that their organization deliver to patients in the form of improved quality of healthcare at lower cost (Porter, 2010; Porter, Pabo, & Lee, 2013). The greatest opportunity for lowering costs without sacrificing quality, safety, or outcomes is gained from helping clinicians intelligently reengineer their clinical and administrative processes (Hoffman & Emanuel, 2013). One tool to fill the gap in new services is time-driven activity-based costing, or TDABC (Kaplan & Anderson, 2007). Using TDABC enables providers to accurately measure the costs of treating patients for a specific medical condition across a full longitudinal care cycle. It uses two proven management tools: process mapping from industrial engineering, and activity-based costing from accounting.

Clinical teams direct the process mapping component and identify the high-level events in a care cycle to describe all the clinical and administrative process steps involved in a patient's complete cycle of care. This provides the data for clinicians and administrators to collaborate on cost reduction and process improvement projects (Kaplan et al., 2014). Although patients have been viewed as consumers of healthcare services since the 1970s (Hutton, Leung, Mak, & Watjatrakul, 2011), the field of hospital marketing is still in its infancy. Today, healthcare management is looking for approaches to overcome the obstacles of growing consumer and market pressure. As market-driven planning positively affects profitability, growth, and patient retention of healthcare providers, hospitals are increasingly adopting a patient-focused marketing orientation (Huang, Weng, Lai, & Hu, 2012). Despite unplanned, infrequent, high-involvement, and high-risk situations when making medical decisions, and lack of knowledge to judge treatment quality, patients are more active in health-related decisions than ever before (Hogan, Oswald, Henthorne, & Schaninger, 1999).

The speed of inter-connectivity of online media have led to the emergence of an entirely new, fragmented portfolio of information channels available for healthcare information (Hennig-Thurau et al., 2010).

Healthcare consumers can access information on the latest medical diagnosis and treatment options immediately online and interactively exchange medical experiences in online communities (Kneeling, Khan, & Newholm, 2013). This improved access to health information leads to an empowerment of patients as health consumers (Rust & Ezpinoza, 2006). As health information and public awareness increases, patients are more knowledgeable about health providers and services than ever before (Revere & Robinson, 2010).

Today, hospital marketers search for strategies that pull patient to them instead of pushing their message out to passive recipients. Selling healthcare services is a complex endeavor and differentiation within comparatively strong markets is hard to achieve.

On the one hand, continuous consumer-centeredness of healthcare systems leads to a race for patients and increasing importance of marketing in healthcare organizations (Kay, 2007; Kotler, Shalowitz, & Stevens, 2008). Fueled by the economic growth of the healthcare sector, marketing research within this area is accelerating (Crie & Chebat, 2012). Patients are becoming more educated on the quality data needed to appropriately assess and evaluate the differences in quality efforts that exist between many organizations (Coates, 2010).

The increasingly competitive environment is having a strong bearing on the strategic marketing practices of hospitals (Revere, Robinson, 2010). In developing distinctive competitive competencies, many healthcare providers are placing quality of care at the core of their marketing strategies (Rubin, Pronovost, Diette, 2001).

As the digital health revolution continues to unfold, electronic data flows from nearly every direction of a patient's health journey, from electronic health records to billing systems, prescriptions, social media, wearable devices and smartphone apps. Hospital Marketers can use this data to get actionable insights about their patients, improve quality of care and patient outcomes. Also, marketers and health care professionals can use artificial intelligence (AI) and patient information to predict certain actions, such as which patients will likely be readmitted to the hospital, which patients are least like to follow through on their prescribed medication regiment, and which patients are most like to manage their chronic disease, and more (Drell and Davis, 2014). Estimates suggest that 78% of Americans use the internet and over 58% use it to obtain health information (Atkinson, Saperstein, & Pleis, 2009; Zichur & Smith, 2012). As the use of social media rises, hospitals are adopting effective social media strategies that are leading to improved patient recruitment, retention and income (Richter, Muhlestein, Wilks, C. E. A., 2014).

Research indicates that social media can benefit organizations in two primary ways: (1) audience engagement and communication for market insights and information dissemination.

Another area of strategic aggressiveness for hospitals is management strategies that can influence the success and profitability of a healthcare organizations. In response to these challenges, healthcare executives must implement management strategies that will enable them to optimize investments in human capital to sustain a competitive advantage. Two archetypal management strategies are autocratic and participative management strategies endeavor to increase employee productivity by rewarding performance, fostering employee commitment, and decentralizing decision making to give employees more voice in work decisions.

Numerous challenges confront managers in the healthcare industry, making it increasingly difficult for healthcare organizations to gain and sustain a competitive advantage (Angermeier, Dunford, Boss, 2009). The other component of strategic aggressiveness is implementation of new healthcare technology. The development and implementation of Electronic Health Records (EHR) is a healthcare product that hospitals have adapted into their database systems to reduce costs and improve efficiency (Diana, Harle, Huerta, Ford, & Menachemi, 2014). Electronic health records can improve the performance of hospitals by identifying and preventing harmful drug interactions or allergic reaction. Also, EHR can assist physicians manage patients with complex chronic conditions and increase efficiency by eliminating medical transcription and reducing duplication of diagnostic tests (Ginn, Shen, Moseley, 2011). Electronic health records will continue to expand to all areas of hospitals and healthcare organizations. Another innovative product, healthcare organizations use is virtual healthcare systems (Telemedicine). Virtual healthcare has changed the way healthcare is delivered by allowing a patient to see a healthcare specialist by e-visit or telehealth online at any time of day. This reduces cost of care by cutting travel, eliminating wait times, and increasing the productivity of the providers (Grube, 2015). Many hospitals and healthcare systems are implementing innovation centers within their hospitals to address the next generation of technology and tackling some of the hospital's biggest challenges (Barnet, 2015). The recent pandemic accelerated the use of telehealth visits. Another area of strategic aggressiveness is healthcare marketing. Healthcare organizations need marketing strategies that capitalize on consumer internet behavior and information needs. Hospital executives must understand the importance of developing a marketing strategy that matches the organization's mission, vision and goals. Healthcare organizations have a variety of marketing strategies that they can use to fit their organization.

Some of the marketing strategies include a market-oriented strategy that focuses on the market and competition to increase the organization's market share. Another marketing strategy is marketing mix strategy that focuses on services, price, place and promotion of the hospital (Thomas, Calhoun, 2007). Also, marketing via the Internet must be viewed as an essential component of a healthcare organization's marketing strategy (Revere, Robinson, 2010). Using quality care as a marketing strategy requires healthcare organizations to determine how consumers perceive and assess quality. One of the key tasks for healthcare marketers is increasing or improving the consumer perception of the organization's quality and using the internet is a perfect tool for accomplishing this task (2010). Another marketing strategy that hospitals are using is social media that has shown to increase revenue, employee recruitment, and customer satisfaction when used effectively (Richter, Muhlestein, Wilks, 2014). Hospitals have found success in social media implementation with minimal resource expenditures that has generated millions of dollars in additional revenue.

The potential targeted audience reached with Facebook & Instagram posts, Snapchat, Twitter (X) tweets, YouTube videos is immense. Research indicates that social media can benefit organizations in two ways: (1) increased audience engagement and communication for market insights and information dissemination (Richter, et., 2014). Healthcare organizations recognize competition is a powerful tool in optimizing costs and quality in healthcare. Competition will require unpalatable changes to the healthcare system to decrease costs without further restricting access or decreasing quality (Kellis, Rumberger, 2010). The increasingly competitive environment is having a strong bearing on the strategic aggressiveness of hospitals (Revere, Robinson Jr., 2010). Studies show that consumers seek knowledge not only about disease and health, but also about providers, services, and quality.

In developing distinctive competitive competencies, many healthcare providers are placing quality of care at the core of their marketing strategies and how consumers determine the level of quality of a healthcare organization is crucial in the consumer decision-making process. Facing increasing competition, hospitals are engaging in merger and acquisition behavior to increase their market share and become more competitive (Creswell & Abelson, 2013).

Capability Responsiveness in the Healthcare Industry

Capability responsiveness in the healthcare industry can be defined as the climate, in which management will tend to respond to turbulence in the environment; competency is management's ability to respond to turbulence in the environment; and capacity is the volume of work that management can handle. Numerous challenges confront managers in the healthcare industry, making it increasingly difficult for healthcare organizations to gain and sustain a competitive advantage. Thus, healthcare organizations must examine their personal management strategies to ensure they are optimized for fostering a highly committed and productive workforce (Angermeier, Dunford, Boss, Boss, R. W. 2009). Hospitals understand the importance of keeping quality healthcare workers and are consistently searching for the best and brightest in the industry. Hospital executives know the only way to maintain high-quality service in healthcare is to create a workplace environment where employees are trusted and valued, where communications are constant and clear, and morale is high. That's a tall order in an industry that is rapidly changing and under intense pressure (Goozner, 2014). Many hospital administrators understand that doctor and employee satisfaction drives patient satisfaction and happier employees typically work harder and more efficient.

One area that administrators and managers must improve is their analytical skills and ability to scan, monitor and assess their environments to identify opportunities, threats and trends in the environment to develop sound strategic decisions (Swayne, Duncan, Ginter, 2007).

Governing boards and hospital management play a vital role in the success of a hospital. They are under intense pressure to lead and guide the organization into the future (McDonagh, 2006). Today, the healthcare environment is changing so rapidly that management is having difficulty keeping up with it. Traditional approaches to education for healthcare managers are fallen short in providing healthcare executives with all the tools needed to become fully competent managers. Competencies are typically defined as management's skills, knowledge, and abilities, but attitude is also part of it. Numerous health-related organizations have been developing competency models to determine if healthcare managers meet the standard (Ransom, Joshi, Nash, 2005). Some of the competencies' healthcare managers are expected to have is leadership, management, and professionalism; negotiation skills; as well as organization and planning skills. Other competencies include knowledge of the community & patient rights, regulatory knowledge, political savvy, legal skills, and knowledge of healthcare public policy. Also, data management skills, knowledge of the malpractice process, conflict resolution, problem solving skills, and research knowledge. The additional competencies that healthcare executives need in the current healthcare environment are communication, analytical, flexibility, and team-building skills. These are just some of the competencies needed by healthcare executives to be successful in today's changing healthcare environment (Muglia, 2010). Due to the environment in which nonprofit federal, state, and local hospitals operate, their ability to scan the environment and identify opportunities is limited.

However, many are adopting a more strategic approach to the environment. Community nonprofit hospitals are becoming more strategically aggressive due to all the changes facing healthcare organizations. The responsiveness of an organization's capability should be matched to its aggressiveness and environmental turbulence to optimize the nonprofit hospital's performance. The hospitals with the highest capabilities are flexible and seek to create the environment, in which they operate.

Strategic Success Model

Table 1 illustrates Ansoff's strategic success model. Following an evaluation of an organization's environmental turbulence and strategic aggressiveness, and the responsiveness of the organization's capability, a gap analysis is completed to determine if the organization can meet the demands of the future environment with success. The Strategic Success Paradigm has been validated in many industries and environments, including the banking industry (Lewis, 1989), public works, federal government organizations (Sullivan, 1987), and environmental management systems (Lorton, 2006), but it has not been validated with federal, state, and local non-profit hospitals.

Ansoff and McDonnell (1990) declared that a firm needs to change its competitive posture to be successful in a changing environment. The components of the firm's capability must be supportive of one another (Ansoff & McDonnell, 1990; p. 30). The Strategic Success Model indicates that a given level of environmental turbulence requires a specific level of aggressiveness, responsiveness, and capability from the organization. When there is a difference between what is needed and what exists in the organization, a gap results, and a problem is defined.

This gap is directly proportional to the degree to which the organization falls short of its performance potential. The larger the gap, the greater performance potential is reduced to achieve strategic success. This study leverages Ansoff and McDonnell's Strategic Success Model as a basis for successfully positioning a healthcare organization to be successful in its changing environment.

This empirical research indicated that there is a significant positive statistical correlation between management's perceptions of environmental turbulence and strategic aggressiveness.

In the case of nonprofit healthcare organizations, they exist to provide medical services to patients in need of healthcare. It follows that for nonprofit healthcare organizations to maximize their performance, their strategic aggressiveness, responsiveness, and capability needs to meet the requirements associated with the level of environmental turbulence they experience.

By scanning the environment continuously, healthcare leaders can attain a broader picture of the organization's internal and external environment.

The external analysis will help hospitals understand the changing needs of the patient, community, economy and governmental policies. The internal analysis will provide a wider view of the current state of the organization and the needs of the employees.

Table 1 illustrates the connection between the various levels of environmental turbulence, strategic aggressiveness, and capability responsiveness within the strategic success model.

Strategic Success Model

Environmental Turbulence	Repetitive	Expanding Slow Incremental	Changing Fast Incremental	Discontinuous Discontinuous Predictable	Surprising Discontinuous Unpredictable
Strategic Aggressiveness	Stable Based on precedents	Reactive Incremental Based on experience	Anticipatory Incremental Based on extrapolation	Entrepreneurial Discontinuous Based on expected futures	Creative Discontinuous Based on Creativity
Capability Responsiveness	Custodial Suppresses change	Production Adapts to change	Marketing Seeks familiar change	Strategic Seeks new change	Flexible Seeks novel change
Turbulence Level	1	2	3	4	5

Table 1

Predictability measures the clarity and completeness of a firm's information at the time strategic decisions need to be made. The role of environmental turbulence has been shown to be a key influence on a firm's performance (Westhead, 2004).

In today's market, even nonprofit hospitals face increasing levels of environmental turbulence. Consequently, senior management's perception of environmental turbulence is a key element in studying the healthcare industry's problems.

Two broad categories of environmental variables are the material-resource environment and the institutional environment. The material-resource environment is comprised of four sets of factors: (a) demand factors, (b) supply factors, (c) technologies, and (d) the structure of the industry. Demand factors are irregular and unpredictable. Consumers cannot always readily evaluate the likelihood of obtaining benefits from treatment or even evaluate the appropriateness of their care.

The cost of treatment received is typically paid by third-party payers, so that demand is relatively inelastic, and is insensitive to price differences. Supply factors are those structural factors that affect the supply of medical services in the organization's operating area such as the demand factor. The supply factor also fails to conform to an idealized competitive market in many important ways. Until recently, most U.S. physicians followed the technological imperative—the belief that every physician in every hospital should have available for his or her patients all the technologies of medicine, regardless of cost, questions of priority, or the optimal allocation of resources. For years in healthcare an emphasis was placed on acute care services rather than preventive measures. In today's healthcare environment, preventive care, cost reduction treatments are one of the primary focuses of healthcare organizations across the country.

In a dynamic healthcare market, the strategies required for success in healthcare organizations is changing expeditiously and organizations will need to measure their long-term progress toward achieving their goals and make critical adjustments to their strategies. Strategic metrics and triggers are diagnostic tools used to appraise an organization's performance and reassess a dynamic market (Gish, 2002). Strategic metrics monitors the organizations short-term performance related to the implementation of its long-term strategies that can be externally or internally driven.

External metrics include an organization's market share, relative cost position, patient satisfaction and performance against benchmark quality indicators. These metrics reflect the healthcare organization's performance compared with its competitors. Internal metrics can include physician-recruitment targets, financial performance targets and process-related metrics.

Strategic measures should monitor the organization's overall progress as compared to other healthcare organizations. Healthcare managers need to clearly understand all the metrics and triggers for their measurement. Also, understand that some metrics will require different periodicity of monitoring. For example, some metrics require monthly monitoring, while others may need to be examined less frequently. Some of the key financial metrics for evaluating strategic success in a healthcare organization could be measuring operating margin, debt-to-capitalization, and debt-service coverage. Other measures for long-term success might include market share; patient, employee, and physician satisfaction; cost per adjusted discharge, volume for targeted services; and clinical outcomes (2002).

The technological factors rely heavily on medical technologies of all sorts, including highly specialized personnel and elaborate diagnostic treatment equipment to achieve desired outcomes—in particular, reduced pain, improved functioning, and prolong life. Medical markets vary greatly, even in the same geographical region, in terms of distribution of providers and the concentration of service organizations. Institutional factors are composed of regulatory, normative, and cultural factors that provide coherence, meaning, and stability to the industry. Institutional factors contain a variety of components such as material resources and governance. These influence the hospital industry's changing environment.

In the 1990's, rural hospitals were closing at an alarmingly high rate due to poor financial performance, which caused an adverse effect on the access and financial health of communities served by the closed hospitals. Legislation enacted as part of the Balanced Budget Act (BBA) of 1997 authorized states to establish State Medicare Rural Flexibility Programs (FLEX Program), under which certain facilities participating in Medicare could become Critical Access Hospitals (CAHs).

One goal of the FLEX Program was to improve the financial viability of small rural hospitals. Unlike other small hospitals that receive Medicare payments, CAHs are reimbursed at 101% of allowable Medicare costs. In June 2010, there were over 1,306 CAHs in the U.S., which represented almost 80% of all small rural hospitals and over 60% of all rural hospitals. By most accounts, the CAH payment method and Flex program, improved the financial health of participating hospitals and improved efficiency (Holmes, Pink, 2012).

Communities across the nation depend on critical access hospitals (CAH) to deliver essential care to patients. The success or failure of CAHs depends not only on their operational performance, but also, on their financial performance, which include cash flow margin; days cash on hand, debt service coverage, long-term debt to capitalization, Medicaid and Medicare outpatient cost to charge ratio. In a 2011 study, Kirk, Holmes, and Pink interviewed 19 of the top-performing hospital CEOs and CFOs and developed nine strategic success factors that were common to all. The nine strategic success factors were the knowledge and use of their board of directors, meeting the needs of the physicians, taking strategic planning seriously, obtaining the most revenue for the services provided. Other strategic success factors included continually looking for cost-reduction opportunities, delivering services that the community needs and wants, taking advantage of network affiliations, communication, holding people accountable, and maintaining good CEOs and CFOs.

These indicators were drawn from the CAH Financial Indicators Report, an annual report developed to provide

CAHs with comparative financial information that can help them achieve performance excellence (Kirk, Holmes, Pink, 2012).

These nine strategic success factors are not an exhaustive list of all that's required for a CAH to achieve strategic success or exemplary financial performance but does provide a baseline for the superior financial performance of nonprofit hospitals.

Another area of hospital success is patient satisfaction. The patient-physician relationship is the cornerstone for quality of health care. The Hospital Consumer Assessment of Healthcare Providers and Systems (HCAHPS) survey has provided publicly available data pertaining to patients' hospital experiences and its impact on patient outcomes. Also, it's important because of the role in influencing overall patient ratings of the hospital. Patient perceptions and overall ratings of the inpatient experience have emerged as important indicators of hospital performance. Value-based purchasing (VBP) provides financial incentives for hospitals to improve HCAHPS scores and to maintain good scores (Elliott et al., 2010). Hence patient ratings of the hospital experience are an aspect of care that can potentially influence the hospital's livelihood. Pay-for-performance initiatives will become less tied to technical competencies and more to the quality of patient-physician interactions (Safavi, 2006b). Given patient expectations, the potential for financial penalties and the negative impact that poor physician communication can have on a hospital's public image is crucial for hospitals (Al-Amin, Makarem, 2016). In a recent study of over 2,700 hospitals, the best-performing hospitals reported that physicians communicated well with their patients and had higher HCAHPS scores. Given the impact that value-based purchasing could have on hospital's financial performance and the impact that public reporting could have on patients' choice of hospitals, patient satisfaction with physician communication is a key area for hospitals.

A direct relationship between patient satisfaction and hospital financial performance was formalized in fiscal year 2013, when the Centers for Medicare & Medicaid Services (CMS) introduced the Hospital Value-Base Purchasing Program, which rewards or penalizes hospitals based on several performance criteria. CMS uses a hospital's score on HCAHPS to determine its Medicare pay rate for inpatient care (Butcher, 2015).

MISSION, VISION, AND GOALS OF HOSPITALS

Healthcare is a rapidly evolving industry where hospitals face constantly changing conditions and an ever-increasing demand for services. As the industry changes, hospital administrators must develop concrete mission & vision statements and set goals for the healthcare organization that balance the wishes of their stakeholders with the needs of their customers to improve performance.

Boards, executives and clinical leaders need to ask themselves whether their guiding statements are sufficiently focused and reflective of stakeholder needs to inspire action toward a sustainable future for the organization and those it serves. If not, revisiting the mission and vision to ensure they focus the organization on the right work going forward can help build momentum for change by creating a clear picture of what the organization is striving to achieve (Totten, 2014).

Mission and vision statements are the foundation on which any hospital operates and provides services to its customers. The mission, vision, and goals of a hospital guide the performance of the organization and its employees.

Also, they communicate the purpose of the organization to all the hospital's constituents (shareholders, employees, stakeholders, suppliers).

The goals of the organization provide guidelines for what the hospital is trying to achieve (Friedman, 2000). For years, the healthcare industry lagged behind other industries in the understanding and effective use of the mission, vision, and goal statements of an organization, but healthcare leaders now understand that these constitute the cornerstone on which they operate. One Medical Center's President stated, "Articulating an organization's vision is the single most important aspect of the strategic planning process" and that the vision statement of a hospital clearly drives the organization's strategies, plans and performance (Robinson, 2016).

In expressing an organization's purpose, a mission statement should be consistent with the organization's values and vision. Also, it should be compatible with the organization's strategic ideas and distinguish it from others in its market. A clear mission and vision statement can provide a conceptual bridge from the present to a desired and realistic future (Luke, Walston, Plummer, 2004).

Mission statements should reflect an organization's positive history and traditions, management preferences, distinctive competencies and resources, and existing or attainable competitive strengths. Overall, the mission and vision statements should be mutually supporting and direct the strategy of the organization. Hospital administrators, CEOs, and directors of healthcare organizations face drastic changes in reimbursement, legislation, technology, and other external factors, but it is essential that they have strong mission and vision statements and goals to keep them focused (Forehand, 2000).

Mission and vision statements are the backbone of a healthcare organization and provide the reference point for strategy development, goals, objectives, and standards for employees and stakeholders (Zuckerman, 2000). Zuckerman emphasized that while the mission of an organization should be timeless, the vision should be bound by time (p. 297).

A hospital's mission and vision statements, and strategic goals, must be aligned with its stakeholders, employees, and management to have an impact on the hospital's performance. When the mission and vision statements and strategic goals are not aligned with hospital stakeholders, employee and management performance seems to remain stagnant or decline.

FORCES AND TRENDS IN THE HOSPITAL INDUSTRY

The Affordable Care Act (ACA) enacted in March 2010 was implemented to address critical issues in healthcare, including access to health care, efficiency of care delivery, quality of patient care, and health outcomes (Murray, 2013). Healthcare reform was brought on by the ACA; U.S. hospitals and health systems were confronted with the emerging changes in reimbursement rates from fee-for-service to value-based purchasing (Standard & Poor's, 2013). The ACA required the Secretary of the Department of Health and Human Services (HHS) to establish a value-based purchasing program for hospitals treating patients with Medicare (CMS, 2012). In compliance with this regulatory requirement, the Centers for Medicare & Medicaid Services (CMS) initiated the Hospital Value-Based Purchasing (HVBP) Program (Spaulding, Zhao, & Haley, 2014). This program provided incentive payments to over 2,900 U.S. acute-care hospitals to reward their improved quality of inpatient care to Medicare patients (CMS, 2013a; James, 2012).

The incentive payments were linked to hospitals' performance and improvements in performance relative to a baseline according to a set of quality measures (James, 2012). The quality measures were related to "how closely best clinical practices are followed, and how well hospitals enhance patients' experience of care during hospital stays" (CMS, 2013a, p.1). The trends that have been transforming healthcare in recent years will continue. Other trends changing healthcare are consumers' increasing demand for quality, convenience and responsiveness in healthcare systems; increasing numbers in the elderly population; consolidation and integration of healthcare delivery among hospitals and physicians.

The inexorable shift from volume to value as more providers embrace the principles of the Institute for Healthcare Improvement's Triple Aim and population health. Also, the rapidly expanding growth of the digital and biotechnology field has dramatically improved patient care (Morrison, 2017). Based on the current trend in healthcare cost increases, spending will continue to rise over the next decade at an average annual rate of about 4.8%, and a total increase in hospital spending of 31% over the next several years. Incorporating patient-centered care into healthcare designs signaled a shift in control and power from the hands of the healthcare providers to the patients (Berwick, 2009).

The total increases in healthcare spending will cause a resurgence in managed care that will reduce the growth in hospital expenditures. Other trends in the hospital industry are the increased demand for hospital beds as the population continues to age and more home health services are being offered and demanded (Shactman, Altman, Efrat, Thorpe, & Doonan, 2003).

Medical Technology is changing the healthcare delivery system and forcing executives to change the way they look at their processes. New points of care delivery are evolving, with specialty kiosks, wearable devices, telemedicine, and employer-based or retail clinics connected to electronic health records. In addition, automation of care is developing rapidly by means of artificial intelligence and mobile computing (McLaughlin, Militello, 2015). There has been an increase of medical specialty services offered at small outpatient clinics and the increase of vertical integration and strategic alliances with large healthcare organizations (Scott, Ruef, Mendel, & Caronna, 2000).

The external forces having an impact on the healthcare industry include innovative technologies such as wireless body area networks, which provide a means for low-powered sensors, affixed either on the human body or in vivo to communicate with each other and external telecommunication networks (Rangarajan, 2016). Other changes include new healthcare systems, AI, medical tourism, and increased demand for healthcare services, pending changes to the Affordable Care Act, new regulations, increased competition and mergers (Griffith, White, 2011). Other factors affecting the healthcare industry include more consumer and physician power, lack of qualified nurses and high-tech workers in hospitals, and a decrease in specialized services (Anderson, Rice, Kominski 2001). Hospital cost continuous to be the highest of all industrialized countries, but lack quality of care of other nations. There is general agreement that healthcare and hospital costs are likely to continue to rise in the foreseeable future.

Many analysts have cited controlling healthcare costs as a key tenet for broader economic stability and growth. Former President Obama made cost control a focus of healthcare reform, but it has done little to control cost.

Although Americans benefit from many of the investments in healthcare, the rapid cost growth, coupled with an overall economic slowdown and rising federal deficit, is placing great strains on the systems used to finance healthcare, including private employer-sponsored health insurance coverage and public insurance programs such as Medicare and Medicaid. This is the reason Medicaid has adopted a pay-for-performance program to help reduce cost and improve quality of care.

Federal healthcare spending is another area of concern as healthcare cost continues to rise. In 2012, the Congressional Budget Office (CBO) predicted that federal spending on healthcare growth will grow to just 3% faster than the gross domestic product, but Medicare spending will continue to increase annually. Also, under the ACA, Medicaid spending will continue to grow until a change in policy is enacted. Government programs such as Medicare and Medicaid account for a significant share of healthcare spending in the public sector. Medicare will remain the largest category of healthcare cost accounting for over $616 billion and Medicaid spending over $517 billion (Zigmond, 2015).

Hospital spending growth slowed by half a percentage point to 4.6% in 2010, reaching $794.3 billion, but in 2015, hospital expenditures grew to 5.6% to over $1.036 trillion. By 2021, it was $1.3 Trillion. This faster growth rate reflects increases in service use due to the coverage expansions under Medicaid and private insurance, partially offset by lower Medicare payment rate increases for hospitals mandated by the Affordable Care Act. Hospital spending is projected to grow by 5.8% per year during the period of 2016–2025 (NHE Fact Sheet). Hospital costs have continued to be the highest percentage of healthcare costs, accounting for more than 31% of all healthcare costs. Due to the pandemic there was massive growth in hospital cost that reached $1.3 Trillion.

Expenditures for medical assistance payments represent about 94% of all Medicaid outlays and increased by 7.3% to $339 billion in 2008.

In 2015, Medicaid spending grew by 9.7% to over $545 billion in 2015. Over the next 10 years, expenditures on benefits are projected to increase at an average annual rate of 5.6% and reach $673.7 billion.

There are 2,978 nonprofit hospitals and 1,003 state and local government hospitals, which account for over 60% of all hospitals in the United States (AHA statistics, Jan 2017). Nonprofit community hospitals have an operating expense of over $120 billion and state, local government community hospitals have an operating expense of over $64 billion, which make up between 96% and 98% of their expenses.

The healthcare industry faces several challenges in today's turbulent environment. Some of the issues affecting the healthcare environment include mounting pressures to reduce healthcare spending, increase community health, improve patient care quality and efficiency, and meet all the patient's care expectations. Other issues include changing demographics, an aging population, increased competition from HMOs, globalization of healthcare, and medical tourism (Coile, 1986). Due to skyrocketing hospital costs, increasing public demand for more efficient and better-quality healthcare at lower cost is forcing hospitals to make changes. Other issues affecting the healthcare industry are internet-based medical websites, strict governmental regulations, and expanding treatment options (Butler & Caldwell, 2008).

Another major concern for lawmakers is the skyrocketing premiums and coverages for businesses and families under the Affordable Care Act. The former President made campaign promises that they would repeal and replace the Affordable Care Act with a more affordable and cost reduction plan, he failed to get the bill passed in the Senate. With no alternative in place, premiums for families and businesses will continue to increase.

Under the tax bill passed by the U.S. House and Senate in December 2017, it will eliminate the penalties paid by people who fail to have health insurance required by the ACA's individual mandate. Based on CBO projections, this will cause increases in insurance premiums and the number of uninsured resulting in higher healthcare costs (Blumenthal, D., 2017).

Hospital Stakeholders

Stakeholders play a significant role in the operation and execution of an organization's mission. Stakeholders are any group or individual that have influence on or be impacted by an organization (Brown & Moore, 2001). Stakeholder groups can include staff, volunteers, donors, governmental offices, activists, patients, and the board of directors. The primary internal stakeholder groups are management, staff, board of directors. They have influence on the mission, vision, and goals of an organization. These groups believe in the purpose of the organization but may have different ideas about how to effectively deliver on the mission. Patients are the most important stakeholders in a healthcare organization. They expect and demand quality of care. External stakeholders include government regulatory agencies such as the Joint Commission, State Licensing Agencies, Insurance providers, businesses, suppliers, community organizations, and other organizations. Community groups and provider partners are among the other external stakeholders (White and Griffith, 2010). With fewer hospital resources and the realization that health is determined by a variety of physical, social, and environmental factors, the success of hospitals, including their financial well-being, will be greatly influenced by their ability to engage in collaborative partnerships (Hacker & Walker, 2013). The best chance for long-term success of an organization is to have constant communication with their stakeholders.

One problem area Herman and Renz (1998) found was that stakeholders within the same organization measured effectiveness differently. They found that the most effective organizations had top managers and boards of directors, who discovered what the stakeholder groups wanted and then communicated goals and achievements consistent with the organization's goals. Due to all the watchdog websites and other resources readily available, stakeholders expect efficiency, cost reduction, high productivity, and program impact (Brown & Moore, 2001).

Being accountable to so many stakeholders can pose problems, because management and the board cannot possibly meet all their expectations. Minkoff and Powell (2006) found that when for-profit hospitals had more paid staff, and was more flexible, whereas nonprofits with more volunteer workers had a stronger commitment to the cause and were less flexible. In addition, they found that having a board of directors' vision or mission can circumvent the push and pull from various stakeholders. The stakeholders' goals focus on the social impact of patient care, but stakeholders want to prescribe methods to accomplish that goal and therefore are an influential component of the global model of nonprofits (Kaplan, Witkowski, Abbott, Guzman, Higgins, Meara, Feeley, 2014).

HOSPITAL STRATEGIES

Hospital strategy arrived only recently in healthcare as compared to other industries. As what occurred in the business world, heightened market threats caused healthcare's shift to a more strategic focus (Luke, Walston, Plummer, 2004). Hospitals use dozens of different healthcare strategies, but strategy formulation is based on several factors such as the environment of the hospital, the competition, markets, management, and customers/patients.

These factors were first examined by Michael Porter in 1980 as an analytical tool for organizations to develop a strategy to improve their marketing position and competitive advantage (Luke et al., 2004, p. 148). Some of the diverse types of strategies hospitals use include position, pace, and power strategies. Position strategies are based on a hospital's competitive position in the environment and market. The position strategy is derived from Porter's research on positioning in the field of marketing and provides the healthcare organization with a competitive advantage in the market. Example of these strategies are low costs and differentiation. Another type of strategy is known as pace strategy. Pace strategies are based on the action, aggressiveness, and innovativeness of the healthcare organization.

Examples of pace strategies are judo and defense strategies, both of which are based on the competition's position and posture in the market. Also, both strategies are closely tied to the environmental turbulence in the market (Luke et al., 2004, pp. 125 – 130).

Other types of strategies include directional strategies based on a healthcare organization's mission, vision, values, and goals, and support strategies, which include the organizational culture and resources. Value-adding service delivery strategies, which specify the pre-service activities, point-of-service configurations and processes, and after-service activities required by the strategies developed during strategy formulation. These strategies shape the working environment and behavioral norms, reporting relationships and structure, as well as information flows, financial needs and human resource requirements (Ginter, Duncan, Swayne, 2008). Other strategies include the different type of competitive strategies, which assist the organization with gaining a competitive advantage through the selection and management of key variables that is supposed to improve overall performance (Langabeer, 1998).

Other competitive strategies including positioning strategy, pricing strategy, investment strategy, cost leadership strategy, diversification strategy, and product market strategy. Positioning strategy reflects how effectively an organization has positioned itself to compete in the marketplace and describes the use of a narrow or a broad focus on the overall market.

Pricing strategy focuses on the value of a product or service for expressing the value of a product from the seller's perspective based on price. This strategy pushes for higher prices, but with better overall quality and service. Investment strategy focuses on the allocation of resources or investments into fixed capital (i.e. property, plant, and equipment) that supports the organization (Langabeer, 1998). Cost leadership strategy is a low-cost strategy that seeks to increase the number of patients by focusing on internal processes. Diversification strategy reflects either a focused penetration on specific segments of the market or a broadly diffused coverage of the entire market. Another type of strategy is production market strategy, which represents the type of market in which teaching hospitals tailor their service lines based on demographics, financial status and specialty programs (Langabeer, 1998).

Non-profit hospitals and health systems face operating environments that are challenged by a variety of stresses, including declining volumes, demand for inpatient services and limited revenue growth. Also, hospitals are further stressed by the shift from hospital-based care towards care provided in outpatient settings and changes in payment models and payer mix. Strategic capital planning is a vital up-front process that supports a hospital and health system's ability to achieve long-term mission and stakeholder objectives. In essence, effective strategy can harmonize essential elements of the organization's long-term business plan, mission and vision.

Also, support the organizations business plan, reduce financial risk and return on equity for the organization's stakeholders (Wong-Hammond, Damon, 2013). There are several others, but this research will only focus on those strategies related to a more turbulent healthcare environment.

HOSPITAL LEGITIMACY

Ansoff and McDonnell characterized legitimacy as being based on the analysis of the objectives, the constraints, and the power field within each firm (Ansoff & McDonnell, 1990). Ansoff's model is targeted toward for-profit organizations and does not encompass nonprofit and governmental organizations. Based on the book *Institutional Change and Healthcare Organizations*, the authors (Scott, Ruef, Caronna, Mendel, 2000) defined legitimacy as a condition reflecting the alignment of an organization to normative, regulatory, and cultural-cognitive rules and beliefs in the social environment.

Legitimacy focuses on the healthcare organization's cultural framework in relation to its social environment. According to Scott et al. (2000), legitimacy involves three areas: governance structures, professional associations, and public/governmental agencies.

Governance structures emphasize the type of control a healthcare organization uses. Professional associations focus on regulatory programs affecting hospitals. Public/ governmental agencies are the legal authorities that have coercive power over healthcare organizations, such as the Joint Commission on Accreditation of Healthcare Organizations (JCAHO), the American Medical Association (AMA) and the Occupational Safety and Health Administration (OSHA) and others. Accordingly, the community benefits contribute to their organizational legitimacy (Proenca, Rosko, and Zinn 2000). Community benefits include the quantifiable and non-quantifiable assistance an organization provides to its surrounding community.

Recent changes in U.S. national policies and regulations have created an opportunity for hospitals to improve population health (Chok-shi, Singh, & Stine, 2014; Stoto, 2013). Before the Affordable Care Act (ACA) required non-profit hospitals to conduct community health needs assessments with input from public health experts and other community stakeholders (Gale ET AL., 2014). Although many nonprofit hospitals conduct community health needs assessments and develop implementation plans and partner with community stake-holders, but little is being spent on community health improvement (Young, Chou, Alexander, Lee, & Raver, 2013). Effective leadership is the key ingredient in creating a climate and shaping the organizational culture, in which all healthcare staff can consistently deliver safe, cost-effective and quality patient care (Armit, 2015). Organizational culture is defined as the values and beliefs that characterize an organization.

When those at senior levels encourage teamwork and an entrepreneurial culture, this has a positive impact on quality improvement efforts, group learning, and innovative approaches to problem solving and stakeholder satisfaction. Changing patient demographics, mandates to achieve targeted treatment outcomes, quality improvement challenges, regulatory requirements, and missions to provide care in an equitable manner are motivating healthcare organizations to strengthen their cultural competencies (Betancourt, Green, and King, 2008). Cultural competency in healthcare is defined as "the ability of systems to provide care to patients with diverse values, beliefs, and behaviors, including tailoring delivery of care to meet patients' social, cultural and linguistic needs" (Betancourt et al. 2003).

Culturally sensitive care is essential in creating the optimal patient-centered experience; effective patient-provider communication; delivery of high-quality, evidence-based services; positive treatment outcomes; and high patient satisfaction (Gertner, Sabino, Mahady, Deitrick, Patton, Grim, Geiger, Salas-Lopez, 2010).

The number of cultural competencies in healthcare is increasing due to changing demographics, quality improvement and regulatory requirements, equitable care missions, and accreditation standards. Many healthcare leaders point to support from the organizational culture and values as a key to their success (Scott et al., 2000).

For this research, I used parts of the legitimacy strategy focusing on governance structures, organizational culture, and public/governmental agencies to assess the effect of governing boards, hospital culture, and public & governmental agencies on a hospital's strategic posture.

HOSPITAL STRATEGIC POSTURE

A hospital's strategic posture is concerned with the organization's fundamental behavior within the market. Many hospitals face growing competition from physician-owned specialty hospitals, physician offices, ambulatory surgical centers, and rehabilitation centers. Specialty hospitals may be of particular-concern given their typical focus on relatively more profitable service lines (Guterman, 2006). In addition, strategic posture helps the organization position its products and services within a market through one of the market segment positioning strategies.

The hospital industry has shown that for-profit hospitals have been a force to emulate for nonprofit hospitals by becoming more business-like because of sweeping changes in the structure of the healthcare industry and concomitant changes in healthcare policy.

Although the evidence suggests that not-for-profit hospitals have become more business-like and efficient, they have nevertheless differentiated themselves from for-profit hospitals by maintaining a higher level of community orientation (Potter, 2001). Research by Miles, Snow, Meyer, and Coleman (2006) has shown that there are at least four typical strategic postures for organizations based on their strategic position: aggressive, competitive, conservative, and defensive. The aggressive posture is associated with little environmental turbulence. The strategic posture is for healthcare organizations in a relatively unstable environment. The conservative posture is for organizations in a stable market with low growth that focuses on financial stability. The defensive posture is for organizations that lack a competitive product, service and financial strength.

Healthcare organizations can change their strategic postures to match the demands of their environmental context and improve their performance (Swayne, Duncan, & Ginter, 2008).

One critical area of strategic posture for nonprofit hospitals is community orientation, which is defined as a set of activities that health services organizations perform in conjunction with other community institutions to manage community health (Ginn, Shen, & Moseley, 2009). Community orientation for nonprofit hospitals is a way for them to meet the expectations of local government and third-party payers. Proenca (1998) described community orientation as the organization-wide generation, dissemination, and use of community intelligence to address present and future community health needs. Operationally, hospital community orientation means that hospitals engage in activities related to illness prevention, collection and dissemination of community health information, and collaboration with other organizations in the community through mechanisms such as multi-stakeholder alliances (Kang, Hasnain-Wynia, 2013).

It is a means for hospitals to manage their dependence on managed-care organizations and other key stakeholders. Nonprofit hospitals with a high degree of community orientation may be well positioned to design and implement programs, target specific populations through knowledge of their community, identify gaps in care, and align with other organizations' strategies for improving overall healthcare quality. Community-level interventions to improve quality of care are complex and require the involvement of multiple key stakeholders, including providers, insurers, purchasers, and patients. One example is the aligning forces for quality programs that focuses primarily on improving ambulatory care quality. Hospitals that participate are involved in a variety of quality improvement initiatives that range from increasing the role of nurses in improving quality and reducing hospital readmissions and safety, to improving language services for patients with limited English proficiency and increasing the efficiency of hospital emergency departments.

One of the most challenging strategic choices hospital boards and CEOs face is should they maintain their current business model or transform their organization into an Accountable Care Organization (ACO)? The traditional hospital model with providers as the primary customer is in sharp contrast to the ACO's core business of patient care because it encompasses service, quality and cost management, where the primary customers are the patients and payers (Anderson, 2010). These two models represent very different businesses and require wide-reaching changes in governance, leadership, organizational design and multiyear investment in new systems and capabilities. Changing business models is risky for hospital leaders and many are hesitant to change due to financial and market familiarity and stability. Healthcare leaders worry that they could lose ground as competitors continue to invest in upgrading facilities and adding new technologies.

ACOs require the engagement and alignment of a physician network and providers and many may not be as ready to embrace the hospital strategic plan. ACOs require a strong and capable primary care network to manage and coordinate care and experienced business-savvy physician executives, who are considered a rare commodity. Despite these reasons for holding ground in a pure hospital model, board of directors and hospital leadership cannot ignore the compelling cost and quality issues forcing delivery system reform. For nonprofit hospitals, the biggest driving factor is the Centers for Medicare & Medicaid Services' movement for bundled risk-bearing payment systems (2010). Many hospitals are not fully ready to embrace the ACO vision, but many hospitals are investing in their capabilities and systems that strengthen the organization in the current fee-for-service environment while simultaneously building required infrastructure and skills necessary for an ACO. By investing in clinical information systems to connect physicians, hospitals and patients will better position healthcare organizations in the current fee-for-service market while building the backbone of an ACO. An organization can assess its strategic posture by examining its current mission and vision statements, its annual and three-year goals, strategic plan and plans for capital investment, physician recruitment, leadership team recruitment, clinical IT, primary care and approach to payers. These are tangible reflections of strategic intent for any healthcare organization.

HOSPITAL STRATEGIC INTENT

According to Hamel and Prahalad, strategic intent motivates competitive strategy by providing organizations with three essential framing conditions: a sense of direction, a sense of discovery, and a sense of destiny. Strategic intent frames the ideas the organization need to achieve its purpose and serve to motivate employees, inspiring commitment to achieve organizational goals and strategies (Luke et al., 2004, pp. 59-60).

Strategic intent is closely tied to an organization's mission, vision, goals, and strategies. A hospital's strategic intent plays a vital role in allowing it to accomplish its mission in accordance with its vision, and goals. Also, an organization's strategic intent should fit firmly into its social constructs of its legitimacy strategy and not be altogether unresponsive to changing environmental, market, and strategic conditions. On the one hand, they should provide a solid foundation for the strategic decisions of the organization. The formulation of strategic intent should be a joint effort involving board members, management, and employees. This type of collaboration creates "buy in" and gives the statements their best chance of becoming embedded within the culture of the organization (Luke et al., 2004, p. 61). An organization's strategic intent should fit firmly within these social constructs. A hospital's strategic intent plays a pivotal role in facilitating the necessary cooperation among the hospital and the community it serves, its physicians, and employee stakeholders (Ford, Boss, Angermeier, Townson, Jennings, 2004).

HOSPITAL PERFORMANCE MEASURES

The critical question facing healthcare leaders is how to prioritize performance measures in today's highly competitive healthcare environment (Erwin, 2009; Langabeer, 2008; Sicotte et al., 1998). Based on H. David Sherman, there are a few key dimensions of hospital performance measures that include: 1) quality of health care, 2) efficiency of services.

Quality of health can be segmented into the effectiveness of the diagnosis, treatment and patient satisfaction. Efficiency can be segmented into price efficiency, allocative efficiency, and technical efficiency. Accreditation standards assure that hospitals meet some of the minimum quality standards (Sherman, 1985).

There are several efforts now under way, including public reporting, pay-for-performance, and ongoing quality improvement programs aimed at enhancing quality.

Many public healthcare programs now report quality measures that allow comparison of the quality of institutional and provider performance. The Centers for Medicare and Medicaid Services (CMS) produces comparative quality reports on many of its participating providers, including health plans, hospitals, nursing homes and others (2005). Major accreditation and certification organizations such as the Joint Commission have increased requirements for monitoring and demonstrating quality improvements. The Center for Medicare and Medicaid Services have encouraged the development of measures for patient's perception of care.

The magnitude of the various quality improvement initiatives has generated high expectations for the use of valid, objective, and reliable performance measures. All the initiatives, public reporting and others depend on the array of performance measures whose implementation can contribute to realizing the fundamental aims of the nation's health care system to improve healthcare quality for the nation. Efforts to standardize quality and performance measurement and reporting in hospitals have been under way for the past 20 years.

There has been an increasing interest in improving quality and productivity in healthcare sector by adopting lean initiatives (Kollberg, Dahlgaard, and Brehmer 2006; Kim et al. 2009; De Souza 2009; Dart 2011; Knowles and Barnes 2013). In addition, there is a growing interest in using lean management within hospitals to measure success.

While lean has led to performance improvement in many organizations, poor implementation is common. Many healthcare organizations have implemented total quality management without immense success and had the same experience with lean (Joosten, Bongers, and Janssen 2009; Dahlgaard, Pettersen, and Dahlgaard-Park 2011).

The National Committee for Quality Assurance (NCQA), Agency for Healthcare Research and Quality (AHRQ), the Joint Commission on Accreditation of Healthcare Organizations (JCAHO), and CMS have developed a variety of performance measures focused on quality of care standards (2005).

JOINT COMMISSION ACCREDITATION

The Joint Commission and CMS have played important roles in the development of standardized performance measurement and public reporting programs for nonprofit hospitals. In the late 1990s, JCAHO implemented performance measures as a condition of accreditation for hospitals. In 2002, JCAHO introduced a set of standardized core measures into its performance requirements for hospitals (JCAHO, 2005). Hospitals seeking accreditation are currently required to submit data on six standardized measure sets that include Hospital Based Inpatient Psychiatric Services (HBIPS), Perinatal Care, Advanced Certification Heart Failure (ACHF), Advanced Certification Heart Failure Outpatient criteria, Comprehensive Stroke criteria, and Stroke criteria. The Joint Commission integrated performance measurement data into the accreditation process to report on hospital's performance measures. In 2005, CMS began reporting hospital comparative data based on the Joint Commission's performance measures. CMS has played a pivotal role in the development of standardized performance measures for hospitals. In May 2005, the National Quality Form (NQF) established a way to standardize health care quality measurement and reporting by endorsing the Hospital Consumer Assessment of Healthcare Providers and Systems (HCAHPS) Survey. The HCAHPS is to provide a standardized survey instrument and data collection methodology for measuring patients' perspectives on hospital care from the patient's point of view.

HOSPITAL CONSUMER ASSESSMENT OF HEALTHCARE PROVIDERS AND SYSTEMS

Hospital Consumer Assessment of Healthcare Providers and Systems is a core set of questions that can be combined with a broader, customized set of hospital-specific items to improve healthcare services and quality of care (https://www.hcahpsonline.org/home.aspx). With the passage of the Affordable Care Act in 2010 and the move toward value-based purchasing (VBP), hospitals have tried their best to improve their performance ratings, patient outcomes, and hospital efficiency. Although previous research has examined the relationship between hospital characteristics and patient experiences and outcomes of care (Lehrman et al., 2010), few studies have examined sustained superior hospital performance regarding patient outcomes and satisfaction ratings (Al-Amin, Schiaffino, Park, Harman, 2018). In the past few years, measuring, reporting and improving hospital performance on quality of care became a priority for policymakers, payers and hospitals.

Patient ratings of inpatient experiences emerged as a key component of the overall evaluation of hospital performance for both research and reimbursement purposes. The Hospital Consumer Assessment of Healthcare Providers and Systems (HCAHPS) survey was developed by the Centers for Medicare and Medicaid Services in collaboration with the Agency for Healthcare Research and Quality to evaluate patient experiences, provide information to consumers as they compare hospitals, to improve the inpatient care experience. Hospitals are incentivized to perform well on the HCAHPS survey through the availability of patient ratings data to the public and through VBP. Tsai, Orav, and Jha (2015) found a positive relationship between high patient ratings and hospital efficiency and quality.

Previous research has found significant improvements in HCAHPS scores between 2008 and 2011, which indicates that hospitals are responding to financial pressures to improve patients' experiences. The Affordable Care Act shifted the focus on hospital performance from the financial domain to the operational and organizational effectiveness domains, whereby performance is now defined as the ability to manage the health of the population served rather than the volume of services provided. This is the reason the HCAHPS survey was introduced to help measure hospital's organizational performance against other hospitals. Understanding sustained hospital performance on the HCAHPS survey, as well as on measures of patient outcomes, patient safety, and efficiency, is important (Al-Amin, et al. 2016). Although the National Committee for Quality Assurance (NCQA), the National Quality Form (NQF), and the Joint Commission are trying to build a national performance system, one still does not exist (2005).

HOSPITAL FINANCIAL PERFORMANCE

The rate of rural hospital closures accelerated in 2013 and 2014, more than twice the number of closures in 2011 and 2012. Based on estimates of the 47 communities served by these closed hospitals, over 1.7 million people were at greater risk of negative health and economic hardship due to the loss of local acute care services. Many policymakers, researchers, and rural residents are concerned and interested in determining why these hospitals closed and what effects it had on local health care providers and the communities they serve.

Concerns about the financial viability of small rural hospitals led to the implementation of the Medicare Rural Hospital Flexibility Program (Flex Program) of 1997, which allows facilities designated as critical access hospitals to be paid on a reasonable cost basis for inpatient and outpatient services. As the rate of closures diminished, attention to the causes and effects of closures decreased. Although cost-based reimbursement may still provide a protective effect, the healthcare industry is still facing a rapidly changing regulatory and economic environment due to the changes in the federal regulatory policies with the Affordable Care Act (ACA). These additional pressures along with the upturn in closure rates have renewed concern for the viability of nonprofit hospitals in an era of population health, where focus has shifted to quality and value. Rural hospital closures have found that associated factors can be grouped into 2 general-categories: Internal (hospital) and external (market) factors. These factors associated with rural hospital closures include poor financial health, aging facilities, low occupancy rates, difficulty recruiting and retaining health care professionals, few medical services, federal funding, and a small proportion of outpatient revenue. There are many dimensions to a hospital's financial condition, so several financial ratios are commonly needed to assess performance and condition of hospitals. In previous studies, hospital's operating margin, total margin, current ratio, days cash on hand, equity financing, total outpatient revenue and Medicaid & Medicare inpatient and outpatient payer mix have been used to measure a hospital's financial performance (Rundall, Oberlin, Salmon, Thygesen, Janus, 2012).

In a 2009 study, the operating margin and total margin were both significantly lower in closed hospitals compared to open hospitals. Furthermore, the differences were considerable in magnitude between closed hospitals, which had substantial negative operating and total margins, while open hospitals had positive operating and total margins. Also, the current ratio and days' cash on hand were significantly lower in closed hospitals compared to open hospitals. In 2009, closed hospitals had higher debt levels than open hospitals. The equity financing ratio and debt service coverage were significantly lower in closed hospitals compared to open hospitals and open hospitals had a relatively healthy debt service coverage ratio of over 3.35 (Kaufman, Thomas, Randolph, Perry, Thompson, Holmes, Pink, 2016). Furthermore, outpatient total revenue (the percentage of total revenue for outpatient services) were significantly lower in closed hospitals. Also, closed hospitals had lower utilization and occupancy rates than open hospitals. The results of the study were evident that poor financial performance leads to hospital closures. There is some debate over whether improving patient outcomes result in increased hospital's financial return on investment. There are a small number of existing studies that suggest a limited correlation between improved hospital financial performance and improved quality, patient safety, and lower readmission rates. However, these studies had several limitations because they were conducted prior to public reporting of selected outcome metrics by the Centers for Medicare and Medicaid Services (CMS); used data from the Medicare Cost report, which is not uniformly audited and thus prone to measurement errors and uses only relative measures of hospital financial performance, which do not capture the absolute amount of revenue potentially available for investment in quality improvement (Nguyen, Halm, Makam, 2016).

Healthcare delivery in the United states has historically been fragmented, with misaligned financial incentives resulting in reduced care quality and increased costs. In recent years, accountable care organizations (ACO) were established to address both cost and quality concerns. ACOs intend to reduce costs by increasing the emphasis on primary care and financially incentivizing integrated clinical care, care coordination within and across the continuum of care, and patient engagement with health care providers and other professionals. CMS has since begun to contract with ACOs, mostly through the Medicare Shared Savings Program (MSSP) and the pioneer ACO Model.

Over the years, Medicare ACOs have produced modest financial savings for the Medicare program and marginal improvements in care quality. In August 2015, CMS released the second year of ACO performance data, including financial and quality performance data. According to CMS, this latest year of performance data indicates that Medicare ACOs continue to improve the quality of care while achieving cost savings.

In 2014, ACO programs saved the Medicare Trust Funds over $460 million (an increase of $82 million from 2013), with the MSSP ACOs generating $345 million. The long-term success of ACOs is tied to their quality and financial performance. ACOs are only required to report quality performance metrics to CMS, while in the second year ACOs must meet or exceed the quality metrics to fully share in any savings. For nonprofit hospitals to receive reimbursement for the treatment of Medicare patients, hospitals must file the Medicare Cost Report (MCR) annually, which was developed by the Centers for Medicare and Medicaid Services to determine the federal government's share of allowable costs and plays a critical role in determining the hospital's reimbursements.

The report is often used by policy and financial analysts as a primary data source for measures of hospital performance. In one study, the financial measures used were total margin, return on Equity, Current Ratio, Days Cash on Hand, Net days in Accounts Receivable, Equity, Debt Service, and Long- Term Debt to Capitalization, but was not reflected of all hospitals reporting the Medicare Cost Report (Ozmeral, Reiter, Holmes, Pink, 2012). Audited financial statements of hospitals is considered the "gold standard" of financial reporting, which consist of a balance sheet, statement of operations (income statement), a statement of changes in net assets (changes in net worth), and statement of cash flow. In addition, audited financial statements from the American Hospital Directory, a commercial database derived from the Medicare Cost Report was utilized. The financial performance of acute care nonprofit hospitals is most often measured using profitability ratios (Pink et al., 2005). Typically, financial performance measures capture both the revenues and expenses of a hospital, but in one study the researchers used three measures which included: total margin, operating margin and return on assets (Collum, Menachemi, Kilgore, Weech-Maldonado, 2014). Hospitals' ability to grow equity is a key factor in their effort to maintain the up-to-date facilities and equipment needed to attract well-trained healthcare professionals and provide high-quality patient care. For not-for-profit hospitals, retained earnings represent the most important source of equity. Managers of not-for-profit hospitals must focus their efforts to build equity on their organizations internal operations and supplement these efforts with profitable nonoperating activities, including raising capital and managing their financial investments.

Patient care revenue makes up the bulk of a hospital's revenue (McKay and Gapenski, 2009) and effectively managing revenue cycles may reduce the number of uninsured and self-pay patients a hospital serves through improved financial counseling and may consequently lower the hospital's debt and operating expenses. Higher net patient revenue and lower operating expenses results in higher operating and total margins, thus improving a hospital's equity, but hospitals must be able to generate higher amounts of patient revenue to grow their equity. The effective management of the patient revenue cycle has potential to boost hospitals' profitability and strengthen their ability to grow equity (Singh, Wheeler, 2012). In a study analyzing the financial statement of nonprofit U.S. hospitals, the researchers used four measures of hospital financial performance: total profit margin, operating profit margin, cash flow, and hospital equity value. Total profit margin is considered one of the most popular indicators of hospital profitability (Cleverley, Song, 2010). A second commonly used measure of hospital profitability is operating profit margin, which measures profitability solely with respect to patient care services and other operating activities. Cash flow is based on an organization's cash inflows and outflows rather than its accounting earnings. Cash flow plays a key role in estimating a hospital's equity value. As hospitals adopt more aggressive pricing policies and reduce revenue deductions and write-offs, operating revenue per patient increases resulting in higher operating income and higher operating margins. Higher average patient revenue also has a positive, effect on total margin. While operating income represents an important element of net income, the latter also depend on nonoperating activities and financial investment (McCue 2010; Reiter and Song, 2011).

The amount of patient revenue, the speed with which hospitals collect revenue plays a vital role in their financial performance. Shorter collection periods are associated with improved operating and total profit margins. Collecting patient revenues faster reduces a hospital's balance in accounts receivable and, consequently, its need for short-term financing and its interest expense. Reduced interest expense translates into higher operating and net income and improved profit margins. Unlike net patient revenue per total assets, which is more strongly associated with a hospital's operating performance, days in net accounts receivable displays almost equally strong links with both operating and total profitability. These reductions in interest expenses have a direct effect on a hospital's operating performance, but only an indirect effect on its total profitability, this finding may indicate that hospital managers use surplus cash because of shorter collection periods, but also to invest an interest-bearing security, which produce additional investment income and, consequently, increase non-operating income. A second important finding of this study is that effective revenue cycle management is associated with not-for-profit hospitals' ability to grow their equity capital. Generating more patient revenue results in additional cash inflows from patients and third-party payers, which boosts a hospital's cash flow from operations, one of the major components of its cash flow. In the future, hospitals can expect to see cuts in Medicare and Medicaid reimbursement rates and in disproportionate share payments (Singh, Wheeler, 2012).

SUMMARY OF HOSPITAL PERFORMANCE

For the purpose of my research, the performance measures used was based on the Joint Commission Accreditation status and the Hospital Consumer Assessment of Healthcare Providers and Systems (HCAHPS) scores.

Also, the nonprofit hospitals financial information was utilized as a performance measure. The Joint Commission Accreditation status, the HCAHPS star rating scores can be retrieved from the Joint Commission and Medicare.gov websites. The hospital's financial information can be retrieved from the American Hospital Directory at https://www.ahd.com and the Joint Commission's Accreditation results can be retrieved from the website at https://www.jointcommission. org/accreditation/hospitals.aspx. The Hospital Consumer Assessment of Healthcare Providers and Systems (HCAHPS) star rating scores can be retrieved from the website https:// www.medicare.gov/hospitalcompare/search.html

Hospitals have a variety of other performance measures that include: The Healthcare Effectiveness Data and Information Set (HEDIS), Balance Scorecard, Lean Six Sigma measures, and patient safety metrics. I limited the number of performance measures to the Joint Commission Accreditation Standards for Hospitals, the Hospital Consumer Assessment of Healthcare Providers and Systems (HCAHPS) star rating and the hospitals' financial performance measures.

The Joint Commission performance measures are separated by accreditations and certifications. Since the Joint Commission began following performance on quality measures in 2002, the measures followed from year to year have changed as hospitals made progress and raised the bar. The Joint Commission introduced flexible options that allowed hospitals to report performance data on electronic clinical quality measures, chart-abstracted measures or both. The Joint Commission is recognizing accredited hospitals that have assisted them in developing mechanisms to assist other organizations to meet the challenges in accreditation (Chassin, Baker, 20015).

The Joint Commission accreditation can be earned by many types of health care organizations that include hospitals, doctor's offices, nursing homes, office-based surgery centers, behavioral health treatment facilities and home care services (The Joint Commission Accreditation). The accreditation is a recognized nationwide symbol that reflects a hospital's commitment to quality of care, patient safety, and a continuous process improvement designed to help hospitals better serve their patients and communities. The hospital accreditation process goes from an on-site survey to intracycle monitoring to assure that organizations are maintaining compliance. The Joint Commission evaluates hospitals from all settings – community, academic, government-owned, pediatric, long term acute care hospitals, psychiatric and specialty hospitals. The Joint Commission is the only accrediting organization to represent the entire continuum of care with accreditation for all types of hospitals (The Gold Standard in Hospital Accreditation, 2016).

There were 29 accountability measures of evidence-based care processes in 2015 and 2016 that was closely linked to positive patient outcomes in hospitals. The Joint Commission worked with the Center for Medicare and Medicaid to develop the quality measures for hospital accreditation (National

Hospital Quality Measures). The focus for my research was on accreditation for non-profit hospitals. The Joint Commission placed more emphasis on a hospital's performance for accountability measures—quality measures that meet several criteria designed to identify measures that produce the greatest positive impact on patient outcomes when hospitals demonstrate improvement. Accountability measures have already been integrated into the information reported on QualityCheck. com in the National Quality Improvement Goals performance information in Quality Reports. Also, Hospital Compare is a consumer-oriented website that provides information on how well hospitals provide recommended care to their patient.

Hospital Compare allows consumers to select multiple hospitals and directly compare performance measure information. Hospital Compare was created through the efforts of Medicare and the Joint Commission. This research utilized the Joint Commission's hospital accreditation performance measures as one of the tools in assessing the hospital's performance. The other measurement tools was the Hospital Consumer Assessment of Healthcare Providers and Systems Survey and the hospital's financial performance. The Center for Medicare and Medicaid (CMS) initiated making payments to hospitals based on their HCAHPS scores as part of the Hospital Value-Based Purchasing program. Since 2008, HCAHPS has allowed valid comparisons to be made across hospitals locally, regionally and nationally (CMS, 2015d, p.1). Because scores of each hospital are publicly available to healthcare consumers,

HCAHPS has enforced the need for hospitals to evaluate their quality of care from the perspective of patients (Frampton et al.,2008).

Hospitals that maintain high HCAHPS scores "can attract more patients, providers, and payers" (Bisognano & Kenney, 2012, p.206). The HCAHPS Survey has eleven measures that are publicly reported on the Hospital Compare website at www. medicare.gov/hospitalcompare or http://www.hcahpsonline.org/ StarRatings.aspx. Hospital care accounts for the single largest category of national healthcare expenditures, totaling $936.9 billion in 2013 and over $1.07 trillion in 2016 and $1.3 Trillion in 2021. With ongoing scrutiny of U.S. healthcare spending, hospitals are under increasing pressure to justify high costs and robust profits (Nguyen, Halm, Makam, 2016). Hospitals are multiproduct firms, with multiple sources of revenue. They provide inpatient and outpatient health care services and provide other services relating to the hospital such as (parking, cafeteria, laboratory, imaging services).

There are three common measures of margins for nonprofit hospitals: total margin, operating margin and patient care margin. Total margin is total revenue from all sources minus total expenses divided by total revenues from all sources. Operating margin is only revenues from operational activities and expenses associated with nonoperating revenues subtracted from expenses (both inpatient and outpatient services) before taxes. The third frequently used measure is patient care margin, which only considers revenues for patient care services compared with operating costs for patient care services (Needleman, 2014).

Nonprofit hospitals use fund accounting and are guided by accounting principles for hospitals or accounting policies for governments, which own them. Based on prior research, Non-profit hospitals act similarly to for-profit hospitals in fiscal management to maximize returns from their investment in capital projects such as buildings, land, and equipment (McCue & Thompson, 2010). Nonprofit hospitals depend on debt financing, in addition to cash flow and philanthropy, to fund these investments because they have no ability to issue stock. Credit rating agencies such as Moody's Investors Service and Standard & Poor's use a variety of factors to determine bond ratings. These factors are linked directly to the hospital's financial performance. Solovy in 2006, theorized that despite the growing interest in quality and uncertainty that hospitals with better clinical outcomes, patient experience scores and efficiency are likely to experience improved financial performance given the shift toward pay-for-performance reimbursement models. Nonprofit hospitals do not have profit-maximization objective, but their motivation is for tax-avoidance and financial sustainability (Dong, 2016). A hospital's poor financial condition can lead to it closing or reducing the services and quality of care it provides (Bazzoli, Fareed, Waters, 2014).

Non-profit hospital's financial viability can be attributable to operating profit margin, total margin, return on equity, return on assets and cash flow margin. Total margin and operating margin has been widely used in studies as a measure of hospitals' overall profitability and performance (Burkhardt & Wheeler, 2013). Based on Becker's Hospital Review in 2017, the average operating and total margin for nonprofit hospitals was 3.4 percent and Return on Assets and Equity was 4.8 percent. While the median cash flow margin for nonprofit hospitals was at about 10% or higher (Ellison, Cohen, 2017). Other financial indicators are the total liquidity, financial leverage, and profitability, financial viability indicators measure a hospital's ability to generate financial resources required to replace assets, acquire new technology, and meet increasing demands for service (Pink et al., 2007).

Higher amounts of patient revenue collected, and speedier collection of patient revenue are empirically associated with better hospital financial performance measured by operating profit margin, total profit margin, free cash flow, and value of equity capital of hospitals (Singh & Wheeler, 2012). Return on assets is considered one of the key financial performance measures for non-profit hospitals (McCue and Nayar, 2009). Authors Pink, Holmes, Slifkin, and Thompson (2009) developed benchmarks for five financial indicators (cash flow margin, days cash on hand, debt service coverage, long-term debt to capitalization, and Medicare outpatient cost to charge) of U.S. critical access hospitals and identified cash flow margin as one of the four indicators of financial outcomes when compared to other hospitals. In fiscal year 2015, not-for-profit hospitals improved their revenue and profitability margins.

The not-for-profit hospital sector's median three-year revenue compounded annual growth rate of 5.6% and gains in cash flow and investments strengthened liquidity and debt ratios (Daly, 2016).

Positive-equity market returns and slowed capital spending helped liquidity reach 219 days cash on hand, with unrestricted cash and investments at 161 percent of total debt. However, the median growth rate for cash and investments slowed from 11 percent in FY14 to only 7 percent in FY15. There is increased pressure on nonprofit hospitals to improve performance and reduce costs, while maintaining operating margin. In one study, five CEOs of large, acute care nonprofit hospitals suggested that net operating margin is a crucial performance measure for healthcare organizations. The financial performance of hospitals is most often measured using profitability ratios (Pink et al., 2005). A widely used definition of financial performance as any profitability measure that captures both the revenues and expenses of a hospital (Casey, Burley, Moscovice, 2007).

RESEARCH MODEL AND SUPPORTING LITERATURE

*T*his chapter will present a literature review, research questions, hypotheses, and definitions of variables pertaining to the research model of this study. The conceptual and operational definitions of the variables will be given, along with the strategic management framework for the research. Also, this chapter contains a discussion of the strategic success model factors, legitimacy, and organizational strategies of nonprofit hospitals. The chapter includes a discussion of the factors of Ansoff's (1979) Strategic Success Paradigm and its relationship to performance in nonprofit hospitals. This study investigates previous research concerning Ansoff's Strategic Success Model and the performance of non-profit hospitals/ healthcare organizations.

Previous research shared common limitations: differences in environmental turbulence between federal, state, local and public nonprofit hospitals, and differences between strategies and legitimacy in federal, state, local, and public nonprofit hospitals. Past research has neglected the correlation between Ansoff's strategic success hypothesis and hospitals.

The research model depicted in Figure 2 improves on the Strategic Success Model to include legitimacy, hospital strategies, and establishing the relationship between them and hospital performance. Based on Ansoff's (1979) Strategic Success Model, it theorizes that hospital performance will be optimal when there is alignment between environmental turbulence, strategic aggressiveness, and organizational capability. Ansoff's Strategic Success Paradigm has been empirically validated on numerous occasions (Ansoff et al., 1993). Previous studies have addressed economic attributes and variables, while this study addresses the social, political, competitive, and regulatory attributes and variables related to the performance of hospitals. The study evaluates nonprofit hospitals' adaptation to environmental turbulence (Ashmos et al., 2000). Nonprofit hospitals had fewer complex environments because of their lack of competition, but most state and local nonprofit hospitals have several competitors and operate in a more complex environment than it did a few decades ago.

The study's definition of environmental turbulence was similar to the one used by Dr. Ansoff (1987): it meant a rapidly changing and complex environment that required aggressive change strategies. For this study, environmental turbulence for nonprofit hospitals is defined as the complexity of the environment, novelty of change, rapidity of change, and visibility of the future based on government regulations, competition, social needs, composition of the population served, and other external influences.

It is believed that all the hypotheses correlate with each other because they are a vital part of the nonprofit hospital's overall performance. Table 1 presented the characteristics of each of the five levels of environmental turbulence.

RESEARCH MODEL SUMMARY

The research model included the Ansoff Strategic Success Paradigm, hospitals' legitimacy strategies, and hospitals' organizational strategies and their relationships with performance. Figure 2 illustrates the various components and their interactions. It represents a segment of the overall global model. The strategic success paradigm evaluates the nonprofit federal, state, and local hospitals' strategic aggressiveness and their responsiveness capability in relation to environmental turbulence.

The legitimacy was measured in this study to evaluate the impact of societal pressures, governmental regulations, and culture on nonprofit hospital performance. It was expected that there would be a relationship between legitimacy and performance. The next area analyzed is the hospital's strategies and their effect on performance. It is expected that there will be a relationship between hospital strategies and performance.

RESEARCH MODEL

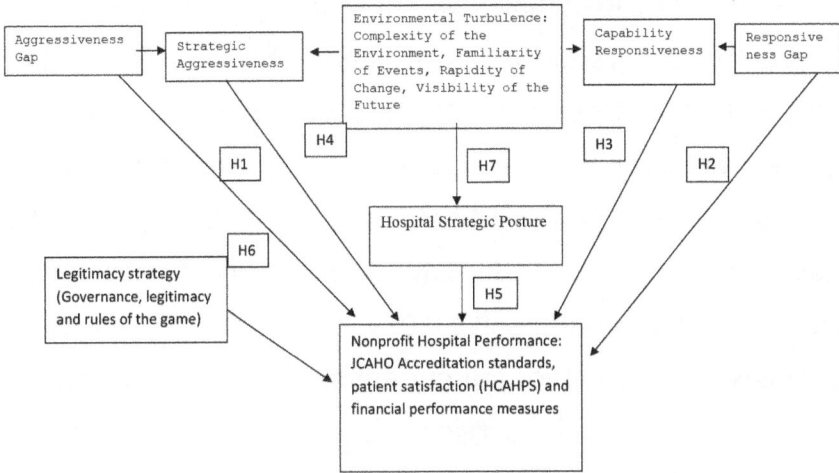

Figure 2. Research model.

RESEARCH VARIABLES

ENVIRONMENTAL TURBULENCE

Ansoff (1979) defined environmental turbulence as the changeability, which includes complexity of the environment and novelty of change and predictability that includes rapidity of change and visibility of the future environment in which an organization operates. Turbulence for nonprofit and federal hospitals is related to social needs, governmental regulations, organizational culture, economic and social change, competitive change, and complexity of the population the organization is serving. Social problems have been considered especially complex and turbulent as nonprofit hospitals are being hit hard with new government regulations and policies, as well as cuts to hospital funding. Governmental regulations can be unpredictable and complex and may change frequently.

Some federal, state and local community nonprofit hospitals have a rapid turnover of employees, which would contribute to greater instability and thus increase turbulence for nonprofit hospitals. The stability and heterogeneity factors used in the definition of turbulence by Galaskiewicz and Shatin (1981) were integrated with Ansoff's (1979) environmental turbulence complexity definition for the current study. Novelty of change refers to changes in services, competition, legislation or technology. Rapidity of change references the speed of changes in services, legislation, technology or competition within the hospital industry. Under the Hospital Readmission Reduction Program (HRRP), for example, the Centers for Medicare & Medicaid Services is reducing payments to hospitals with excess readmissions.

The rise of accountable care organizations (ACOs) and other value-based payment models are being rewarded for delivering high-quality care, which often means pursuing strategies that help patients better manage their conditions and avoid hospitalizations.

Even when hospitals and health systems want to help their communities stay as healthy as possible, the misaligned incentives of the fee-for-service paradigm often have served as a barrier to that goal. ACOs, bundled payments, and programs like the HRRP all designed to reward hospitals for delivering care that keeps patients healthy and out of the hospital.

HOSPITAL STRATEGIC AGGRESSIVENESS

Strategic aggressiveness for nonprofit hospitals is the intention of management to plan, innovate, and develop products and services to meet customer needs in the local community and beyond. Sheehan (1999, p. 417) said that strategic intent was to choose "the future we wanted and set out to make it happen." The one nonprofit he studied showed that setting stretch goals enabled them to push themselves and get results.

A qualitative study by Sawhill and Williamson (2001) of several nonprofit hospitals from various sectors quoted an executive from the American Cancer Society: "It was immediately obvious to all of our staff that business as usual would not get the job done and that we had to be smarter about allocating our resources and more aggressive about trying new strategies" (p. 382).

The aggressiveness of nonprofit hospitals can range from stable to creative and the scale of discontinuity ranges from no change to creative change, which has not been observed previously.

Increased costs of care are attributed to a variety of factors, but most commonly include the costs associated with new technology, innovative therapies, increased demand, and labor required to provide patient care (Bakera, Phibbs, Guarino, Supina, & Reynolds, 2004).

Timeliness ranges from reactive to creative and trying innovative ways to meet patient needs. Nonprofit hospitals can assess their progress about aspirations, strategy, and culture within four levels of capacity. The four levels correspond to: (a) the clear need for increased capacity, (b) a basic level of capacity in place, (c) a moderate level of capacity in place, and (d) a high-level of capacity in place (p. 88). One component of strategy aggressiveness that relates to nonprofit hospitals' strategic aggressiveness is the timeliness of the introduction of new services and technology for the patients.

For nonprofit hospitals, this could be the introduction of cancer treatments or preventive health services. For other hospitals, this could be the introduction of new cardiac services or new mental health treatments. The highest level of aggressiveness for hospitals is their ability to be a leader in developing new cutting-edge technologies and meeting patients' needs. Crutchfield and Grant (2008) studied nonprofits and found that the strategically aggressive nonprofits were those making an impact on the industry by developing and implementing new technology and services to the community. The top performing nonprofit hospitals were learning new ways of interacting to change public attitudes. Their responsiveness to patient needs are creative and revolutionizing the industry rather than just meeting the needs.

It is predicted that some nonprofit hospitals will expand beyond their local areas and have patients from all over seeking their services. Table 1 presents the five levels of characteristics of nonprofit hospitals' strategic aggressiveness as they relate to the five levels of hospital environmental turbulence. If one were measuring the strategic aggressiveness for the nonprofit hospitals studied by Crutchfield and Grant, it would be a five for every characteristic.

HOSPITAL CAPABILITY RESPONSIVENESS

Nonprofit hospitals' capability responsiveness is the way management handles risk and change. In addition, increased risk was positively related to innovation. This is consistent with the corresponding levels of turbulence and organization responsiveness that Ansoff (1979) hypothesized for the Strategic Success Paradigm. When organizations were more strategic and open to risk and change, the organizations anticipated change sought to create new environments. Table 1 summarizes the levels of nonprofit hospital responsiveness that correspond with the levels of environmental turbulence. McKinsey (2001) studied a small number of nonprofit hospitals, but the research strongly suggested that capacity building or having managers build their staff increased social impact.

Ashmos et al. (2000) found that the differing internal make-up of the organizations studied dictated how the hospitals adapted to complexity. Some hospitals organized themselves with fewer goals, formalized roles and rules, and created boundaries despite the complexity. They sought stability and were more risk adverse. Yet the strong performers that responded to complex turbulence with strategic and structural complexity outperformed the other hospitals that responded with fewer goals and risk averseness. Ashmos et al. (2000) found the organizations that were more informal and had decentralized structures accepted risk and changeability more easily.

HOSPITAL LEGITIMACY

Many researchers have provided definitions of organizational legitimacy. Weber (1968) defined legitimacy as the valid domination that is then institutionalized with patterns of offices, rules, or procedures that validate the conformity and devotion of an organization's members.

Bell (1977) argued that legitimacy refers to an institution's extent of authority. Berger (1981) defined legitimacy as the rightful control of power; executives must assure the public that they use their power responsibly. They must command obedience from the members of the organization and support from nonmembers. Ansoff and McDonnell (1990) defined legitimacy in terms of business as the degree of responsiveness of a firm's behavior to its stakeholders' expectations. They described legitimacy strategy as aspiration analysis, the impact of constraints, and the power field analysis of the organization (1990; p. 208). Scott (1995) defined legitimacy as a condition reflecting cultural alignment, normative support, or consonance with relevant rules or laws (Scott, 1995; p. 45), depending on whether the emphasis is on cognitive, normative, or regulatory aspects of the healthcare organization. There are many sources of regulatory authority over hospitals, including common law, labor laws, personnel licensure, monitoring of financial operations, hospital licensure, and Medicaid/Medicare certification.

In his study of hospitals sponsored by the Catholic Church, White stated that "organizational legitimacy is an important part of the survival of hospitals" (White, 2003; p. 87). Founded in institutional theories of organizations, the legitimacy construct refers to the way organizational leaders use symbols to gain internal and external support (White, 2003). White (2003) adopted a broad definition of legitimacy based on such authors as DiMaggio and Powell (1983), Scott (1992), Suchman (1995), and Zucker (1987) by including organizational culture, in addition to symbols, as a method to gain organizational support. He stated, "Legitimacy refers to the way organizational culture exists" (White, 2003; pp. 87-88). This cross-case analysis provides a unique view of legitimacy by explaining the intra-organizational relationship between the leaders of the hospital and culture.

Hospitals are attempting to create a culture that defines itself with the inclusion of all organizational members, or to legitimize their organizations and their role. In terms of healthcare management, the hospital leaders first attempt to legitimize the ability of the hospital to improve the health of community members with its own improvement efforts.

Secondly, hospital leaders legitimize their hospital's role as an influential and key decision maker and goal setter for care management in the organization. And lastly, all hospital leaders legitimize the existence of the hospital as an integrated organization focused on health and wellness of the community. After reviewing Luke and Walston's (2003) concept of a legitimacy strategy model for the framework of my analysis on intra-organizational relationships in nonprofit hospitals. They suggested that even though organizations make rational, strategic choices to gain market power, create efficiencies, and/ or control resources, these rational choices are balanced by institutional constructs.

They identified professionalism (power and control), interdependence (trust), and mission-strategy conflict (goals) as key institutional barriers that influence strategic choices (Luke & Walston, 2003). They suggested that these three institutional constructs influence an organization's mission, strategy, and goals by creating conceived barriers or by reducing strategic options for the organization (Luke & Walston, 2003). The variable power, goals, and trust with the addition of decision making was used to describe the intra-organizational relationship between the hospital leaders as they legitimize their role in the hospital's mission, strategy, and goals.

There are three types of legitimacy: *pragmatic*, derived from stakeholders' self-interest; *moral*, an agreement that the organization does the right thing undergirded by shared values; and *cognitive*, based on either the organization's actions being understandable or taken for granted. Suchman (1995) also argued that gaining, maintaining, and repairing legitimacy operate at various levels and are essentially different processes. Aldrich (1999) agreed with Suchman's definition but collapsed the typology into *cognitive legitimacy* and *sociopolitical legitimacy*, arguing that pragmatic legitimacy was part of organizational learning processes. Both Scott (1995) and Aldrich (1999) viewed cognitive legitimacy the same way that population ecologists do: a signal of shared values that are taken for granted by organization members. Sociopolitical legitimacy is the evaluation by others, including stakeholders, the public, and community leaders, as to the appropriateness of the organization. It is granted through moral acceptance by conformity with cultural values and norms, or through regularity acceptance by conformity to laws. Legitimacy involves normative support for organizational mechanisms such as personnel management, accounting practices, and the rules of conduct and structure of the hospital staff. With respect to hospitals such legitimacy is typically conferred through oversight bodies (e.g., The Joint Commission, AHA, etc...) that review the structure and functions of governance boards and administrative hierarchies.

By contrast, technical legitimacy is focused on aspects of core technology, including normative support for staff qualifications, training programs, work procedures, and quality assurance mechanisms. In the healthcare sector, these assessments revolve around patient-focused tasks such as diagnosis, treatment, education, and continuum of care, as well as ethical standards concerning patient rights (JCAHO, 1996). Most healthcare organizations have traditionally attempted to differentiate structure and insulate the sphere of technical tasks from administrative tasks (Smith, 1955; Goss, 1961). All hospitals have the opportunity to seek legitimacy from a variety of external normative sources. Some of these are more clearly focused on managerial procedures, some on technical procedures, and some pertain to both.

Because managerial legitimacy is typically governed by different societal values (efficiency and cost containment) than technical legitimacy (quality of patient care and specialty training among health organizations), the types of procedures suggested by different normative sources need not be complementary and may even conflict with one another. Quality and performance measures should meet the needs of stakeholders and therefore should include clinical indicators of quality and indicators deemed important by the consumer (i.e. patient survey results, customer satisfaction). Data integrity and quality: The data included in report cards and similar quality reports should be held to the highest standards of accuracy. They should be free of bias and disseminated by an objective third party. All data should be risk adjusted according to a standardized method that is publicized and easy to replicate. Reports should be valid and easy for the average consumer to understand. The data should provide utility to all stakeholders and should be compatible with other quality reports and ratings of comparable institutions. In this empirical investigation, I considered seven sources of normative legitimation, three of which focused primarily on managerial aspects of hospital activities, three on technical aspects, and one of which encompassed both. Hospitals improve their survival chances insofar, as they are successful in obtaining legitimacy from such normative sources such as the Joint Commission on Accreditation of Healthcare Organizations (JCAHO), the Centers for Medicare and Medicaid Services, Agency for Healthcare Research and Quality, and the American Hospital Association (AHA).

The American Hospital Association (AHA) have argued that organizations operating in highly institutionalized environments are more likely to survive to the extent that they are successful in obtaining legitimacy from those normative sources that are able to approve or disapprove their structures, staffing, and programs.

While this proposition should hold true of normative legitimacy viewed in general terms, the salience of managerial and technical dimensions of legitimacy may vary depending on the nature of an organization's environment. Institutional theory defines legitimacy as it relates to the community benefits that hospitals provide. This terminology implies that benefits are measured by their value to the community instead of the cost to the hospital. Costs and values are usually quantified differently, so cost of the benefits and value of the benefits should not be used interchangeably (Byrd, Landry, 2012). Based on research of the different types of legitimacy, my research focused on various aspects of legitimacy in nonprofit hospitals that included organizational culture, management culture, and interdependence.

HOSPITAL STRATEGIC POSTURE

Strategic posture is defined as the approach leaders take in applying their strengths to the current and long-term needs of the marketplace. Formulating a strategic posture is part of the broader strategic planning process, when managers collaborate to develop the vision, goals, and strategies for the future (Kokemuller). Dr. Ansoff defined strategic posture analysis as a descriptive and prescriptive tool used to measure the size of the gap between turbulence, strategy, and capability (Ansoff, McDonnell, 1990). In these times of uncertainty, hospitals and health systems should be actively working on four major strategies to be positioned for the future. These groupings of strategies include: Growth, Effectiveness, Relevance and Capabilities. While growth and effectiveness strategies have been a staple of every health care organization strategic plan over the past two decades, the massive industry turbulence brings into increasing importance the strategies related to relevance and capabilities. It's no longer enough for hospitals to simply drive growth and effectiveness, most hospitals must reinvent their capabilities to remain relevant in light of industry shifts (Lovrien, Peterson, 2013).

Growth strategies are focused on the efforts by the organization to expand their services and ultimately, their revenue and mission. Until recently, growth has been the primary focus for healthcare organizations. Growth strategies take on a number of forms including volume, payor mix, new markets, reputation, size and scale and span of services, and specific populations. Growth is a high-impact, aggressive strategy and is often seen as a sign of strength and success in the American social fabric. Organizations looking to increase margin have two major options: cutting costs and increasing revenue with growth. Increasing revenues with growth has a different effect entirely. Focusing on growth has shown better results than cost savings or even a combination of the two, including a higher return on investment. Growth will often increase the availability of new services and access to existing services, which leads to a loyal and growing customer base. Effectiveness strategies focus on gaining higher value from the organization and delivery of services. Effectiveness has gained increased focus of many healthcare organizations in the last several years as reimbursement and financial pressures have mounted and market volume growth stagnated and shrunk. Key methods toward improving effectiveness from Four of the Top-Performing Hospitals included: Standardizing processes and supplies; improving the coordination of care between handoffs across departments and elements of the continuum; Using technology to complete standardized tasks; reinforcing goals by addressing organizational culture. Approaching effectiveness strategies with an eye toward areas of highest impact now and in the future will cause health systems and hospitals to look at processes both within the hospital and outside the hospital walls. Relevance strategies are strategies that improve the ability to provide services that satisfies the needs of the users. The relevance of health systems and hospitals are being threatened as non-traditional providers are rapidly moving into the provider business.

To remain relevant, health systems must reinvent themselves. This reinvention is particularly important in the case where consumer demands have shifted, technology has created viable substitutes and reimbursement changes the way value is monetized. Some strategies include: Trusted relationships with populations for the coordination of health and care; building primary care and infrastructure to manage the systems of health rather than only the systems of care; customer service strategies such as movement from scheduled (traditional primary care clinic) to on-demand tele-health solutions; delivery channel management and the movement from inpatient to outpatient. Other strategies include leverage of technology to improve access, convenience and costs such as use of online or smartphone apps to deliver primary care diagnosis and treatment; partnerships with non-traditional providers. In a changing world, hospitals will need to better articulate their relevance to their stakeholders, patients, providers, and payors.

Capability strategies focus on developing the abilities and talents needed to coordinate and manage both systems of care and systems of health. In the changing environment of healthcare today, adaptability and innovation need to be a top priority for healthcare organizations. Some examples of capability strategies that health systems might pursue include develop data analysis and population health segmentation models to predict disease and health needs; create care teams to effectively communicate and manage chronic disease through outreach and active care prevention and education; coordinate community outreach and economic development activities to increase the overall health of the population and decrease cost of care; create clinically integrated networks with physician and non-physician providers. Success for health systems and hospitals over the next decade will depend on their ability to balance strategies in the four groupings of growth, effectiveness, relevance and capabilities (Lovrien 2013).

In the presence of a rapidly changing healthcare delivery system, hospitals will likely need to evaluate their community orientation and financing requirements for providing care. Because uncertainty is prevalent throughout the healthcare industry, in part due to uncertainty about medical technology, regulations, political climate; nonprofit hospitals tend to model themselves after similar organizations in the field (Ginn, Shen, Moseley, 2009). Results from a 2009 long-term study of the hospital industry showed that not-for-profit hospitals have been forced to emulate for-profit hospitals by becoming more business-like due to sweeping changes in the structure of the healthcare industry, multiple changes in healthcare policy, and pressure from consumers, and insurers, who are calling for the integration of healthcare quality with broader public and community health objectives. Hospitals with a high degree of community orientation may well be positioned to design and implement programs, target specific populations through knowledge of their community, identify gaps in care, and align with other healthcare organizations' strategies for improving overall healthcare quality in the community.

Hospitals actively engaged in these alliances demonstrate a level of commitment to community orientation by looking beyond the internal factors influencing quality to involve the community. Although the evidence suggests that not-for-profit hospitals have become more businesslike and efficient, they have differentiated themselves by maintaining a higher level of community orientation. Hospitals are concerned with their social legitimacy and the higher barriers for licensing, accreditation, and certifications all attest to the institutional pressure from society due to the importance of the services hospitals provide. Because most hospitals are community hospitals, we assume legitimacy to be primarily a local issue.

The business strategy is manifested in the alignment of a healthcare organization with its external environment. The organization aligns itself by establishing linkages with external parties to secure the resources that it needs to survive and by making internal structural adjustments. For the organization to be properly aligned, its organizational strategy should represent an internally consistent configuration of functional area strategies. Thus, one would expect that an organization strategy in the functional area of finance should be consistent with its overall business strategy (Coddington, Fischer, Moore 2001). Miles and Snow (2003) identified four common configurations: defender, analyzer, prospector, and reactor.

The defender enacts a stable environment and produces only a limited line of products or services. The defender is generally risk-averse and avoids offering new products or services. It develops a core technology that is highly efficient and uses an organizational structure with centralized control. The defender has an internal focus and the prospector is the exact opposite of a defender. The defender enacts a dynamic environment and has a product/service line that is broad and changing. The prospector has an external focus and assumes more business risk than the defender by attempting to be "first to market" with new products and services. The prospector avoids long-term commitments to any type of technological process and develops a divisional structure with decentralized control.

The analyzer is a combination of the defender and prospector strategies. It competes in some stable product service lines, but at the same time searches for new product or service opportunities. The analyzer maintains a moderate level of business risk by waiting to see the experience of others before entering a market.

The analyzer partitions its technology so that it can serve its stable domains with efficient technologies and its dynamic domains with flexible and effective technologies. The analyzer differentiates its structures to accommodate both types of technology.

The reactor is an organization that makes inconsistent managerial choices. As a result, it is difficult to predict how a reactor will compare with the other strategy types on any given dimension. Hospitals use multiple strategies to compete and adapt to their environment. Based on their environment and competition, some small nonprofit hospitals use a competitive market strategy. This type of strategy seeks to establish comprehensive healthcare services within the economic demands of the hospital's community. Another strategy that a nonprofit hospital will use is a population health strategy. In this case, the hospital seeks to establish itself as providing essential services for the health of the community and as an organization that gives the community a competitive advantage in attracting industries that will contribute to the community's economic development (Porter, Olmsted-Teisberg, 2006).

HOSPITAL PERFORMANCE MEASURES

The performance of nonprofit hospitals reflects a large variety of measurement tools to measure performance in these types of healthcare organizations, but one must first analyze the type of healthcare organizations being measured. The types of hospitals and health systems that was analyzed in this study: government, state, local community, and teaching nonprofit hospitals and healthcare systems. The government, state, local community, and teaching nonprofit hospitals included small, medium, and large-sized acute care federal, state, local government and teaching hospitals and healthcare systems.

Mental health/Psychiatric, military and veteran administration (VA) hospitals were exempted from the study.

The nonprofit hospitals types were classified based on the following criteria.

- Nonprofit Community hospitals or health systems are classified as voluntary other or voluntary church-owned nonprofit hospitals.
- Government nonprofit community hospitals or health systems are classified as Federal or state governmental community hospitals and does not include Veteran Administration or Psychiatric or mental health hospital.
- Governmental nonprofit community hospitals or health systems are classified as local government community hospitals or health systems and not classified as a Veteran Administration or psychiatric or mental health hospitals.

The performance measures chosen are based on research of the most common nonprofit hospital performance measures and from previous studies analyzing performance measures of nonprofit hospitals. The performance measures that were analyzed included the Joint Commission accreditation scores that range from accredited with the Joint Commission, accredited with follow-up survey, preliminary denial of accreditation, and denial of accreditation. Accredited is defined as the nonprofit hospital is following all standards at the time of the on-site survey or has successfully addressed requirements for improvement in an evidence of standards compliance within 45 or 60 days following the posting of the Accreditation Summary Findings Reports.

Accreditation with follow-up survey is when the hospital is not in compliance with specific standards that require a follow-up survey be conducted within 30 days to 6 months.

Preliminary denial of accreditation is when there is justification to deny accreditation to a health care organization due to one or more of the following: an immediate threat to health or safety for patients or the public; Submission of falsified documents or misrepresented information, lack of a required license or similar issue at the time of the survey, failure to resolve the requirements of an Accreditation with follow-up survey status; patients having been placed at risk for serious adverse outcomes due to significant or pervasive patterns/ trends/repeat findings, or significant noncompliance with joint commission standards. Denial of accreditation results when a hospital has been denied accreditation and all review and appeal opportunities have been exhausted (JCAHO, 2018).

The Hospital Consumer Assessment of Healthcare Providers and Systems (HCAHPS) rating scores is a national, standardized, publicly-reported survey of patients' perspectives of hospital care. The HCAHPS scores are designed and intended for use at the hospital level for comparing hospitals to each other. HCAHPS survey asks recently discharged patients about aspects of their hospital experience that they are uniquely suited to address. HCAHPS is administered to a random sample of adult inpatients between 48 hours and six weeks after discharge from a hospital. HCAHPS Star-Rating provides consumers with a simple overall rating generated by combining multiple dimensions of quality into a single summary rating score. The HCAHPS summary star rating combines information about different aspects of patient experience of care.

The HCAHPS summary star rating is constructed from the following components. The seven-star ratings from each of the 9 HCAHPS composite measures that include nurse communication, doctor communication, responsiveness of hospital staff, pain management, communication about medicines, discharge information, and care transition.

The HCAHPS summary star rating is the average of the 9 composite measure star ratings, the star rating for HCAHPS individual items, and the star rating for HCAHPS global items. The nonprofit hospital financial performance measures include operating margin, total margin, return on equity, return on assets and cash flow margin will help determine the hospital's financial viability and efficiency.

The Joint Commission accreditation scores for nonprofit hospitals was used as one of the performance measurements to determine quality of care performance. Another was the Hospital Consumer Assessment of Healthcare Providers and Systems (HCAHPS) rating scores to determine overall hospital quality of services. Financial performance was determined by the nonprofit hospital's financial stability and viability. The criteria used for the Joint Commission was each nonprofit hospital's accreditation final performance scores that was obtained through the Joint Commission's website at https:// jointcommission.org/accreditation/hospitals.aspx or at the American Hospital Directory website at www.ahd.org. The other criteria was the nonprofit hospital's consumer assessment of healthcare providers and systems survey (HCAHPS), which measure patient satisfaction rating scores obtained through the hospital compare website at https://www.medicare.gov/hospitalcompare/search.html or the HCAHPS website at https://hcahpsonline.org/StarRatings.aspx.

The criteria used to measure the nonprofit hospital's financial performance was the hospital's operating margin, total margin, return on equity (ROE), return on assets, and cash flow margin. Theoretical and empirical literature was previously reviewed on the financial performance of non-profit hospitals.

Nonprofit hospital's financial performance can be attributable to financial indicators such as operating margin, which is net income divided by total revenue. Total margin is net operating income divided by total revenue times 100 to get a percentage. Nonprofit hospital's return on equity is net income divided by total equity (Assets minus liabilities). Nonprofit hospital's return on assets is defined as net income divided by total assets and cash flow margin is net income + interest + depreciation divided by total revenue.

Theoretical and empirical literature was reviewed on the different nonprofit hospital financial performance measures and five indicators were most frequently reported in healthcare financial management literature from peer-reviewed journals or industry-authoritative sources. Among the five indicators were operating margin, total margin, cash flow ratio, return on equity and return on assets.

Operating margin. Operating margin (OM), measures the control of operating expenses relative to operating revenue (net patient and other revenue). A positive value indicates operating expenses are less than operating revenue, which is net patient revenue minus total operating expense, which gives the net operating income indicating profits solely from a hospital's operations (Nowicki, 2015).

Total margin is a measure of hospital financial performance that measures nonprofit hospital's net operating income divided by their total revenue.

Return on Equity (ROE) focus is on both short and long-term results. ROE is a function of margin multiplied by leverage multiplied by turnover. ROE for nonprofit hospitals is calculated as net income divided by total equity (total assets minus total liabilities).

Return on assets (ROA) is net income divided by total assets and **Cash Flow Margin** is the hospital's net income plus interest plus depreciation divided by total revenue. **Days cash on hand**, which is cash on hand plus market securities plus investments divided by total operating expenses minus depreciation expense divided by 365 days of the year. Another vital financial performance measure for nonprofit hospitals is total debt to net assets, which is total liabilities divided by the total assets minus total liabilities and total asset turnover. Total asset turnover is total operating revenue plus non-operating revenue divided by total assts. A national study of hospitals' financial performance, Younish and Forgione (2005) found that operating income is better than equity as a measure of hospital profitability, which is primarily attributable to ownership type, geographic location, facility size, length of stay, patient mix and teaching status.

Total balance has been used as a sole or joint measure of hospital financial performance in empirical studies published in recent decades. Rauscher (2010) and Singh and Wheeler (2012) investigated financial performance of non-profit hospitals across the United States from 2000 to 2007 using total operating income as one of the indicators. Non-operating profit margins (equals total profit margin minus operating profit margin) of non-profit acute care hospital was examined as part of their financial performance. (AHD indicators 2019) https://www.ahd.com/indicators.php?hcfa_id=0e6ed911d02223 fd12ca9d585a2c3af1&ek=b64693af5f0d71328e6a6f1cd 6128550. Cash flow margin is also an important part of non-profit hospital's financial performance. Cash flow margin is a ratio of the sum of net income and depreciation expense to total revenue (Zhao et al., 2008). Hospitals and healthcare organizations are reluctant to provide comparative data or provide proprietary information on financial performance.

Other possible data source in comparing qualitative data is the Leapfrog Group Quality and Safety Survey (Leapfrog Group on Health, 2007) that utilizes evidence-based hospital information in the areas of surgery volume, mortality by high-risk procedure, process measures, and coding criteria on volume counts. Other nationally recognized organizations that provide qualitative studies include the Institute of Medicine (Institute of Medicine of the National Academies, 2005) and the Agency for Healthcare

Research and Quality (United States Department of Health and Human Services, 2007). Despite the depth and breadth of the information available, professional disagreements exist regarding the comparability of this information. Hospital care is still largely local (Luke et al., 2004) and community expectations are derived from numerous sources in a community. Changing local demographic trends and unique healthcare needs provide the necessary data set for hospital strategic planners (Maiga, Jacobs, 2009). For example, inner-city urban hospitals are challenged with psychosocial issues that dramatically influence pre-natal care and infant mortality. Community expectations coupled with demographic data provide hospital strategic planners with valuable information in determining the status of their organizations (Luke et al., 2004; Mycek, 2004).

Hospital effectiveness is not simply a question about whether the structures and processes of medical care result in clinical improvement of health benefits achieved by patients, but also whether anything is being done to improve the health status of the community through enhancements in the physical, social, and economic environment (Aday, Begley, Lairson, & Slater, 1999).

RESEARCH QUESTIONS & HYPOTHESES

Q1. What is the relationship between the nonprofit hospitals' strategic aggressiveness gap and financial performance?

H1: There is a reliable relationship between nonprofit hospitals' strategic aggressiveness gap and financial performance.

Q2. What is the relationship between the nonprofit hospitals' capability Responsiveness gap and quality performance measures of Joint Commission Accreditation and Hospital Consumer Assessment of Healthcare Providers and Systems (HCAHPS)?

H2: There is a reliable relationship between nonprofit hospitals' capability responsiveness gap and quality performance measures of Joint Commission Accreditation and Hospital Consumer Assessment of Healthcare Providers and Systems (HCAHPS).

Q3. What is the relationship between nonprofit hospitals' capability responsiveness and quality performance measures of Joint Commission Accreditation and Hospital Consumer Assessment of Healthcare Providers and Systems (HCAHPS)?

H3: There is a reliable relationship between nonprofit hospitals' capability responsiveness and quality performance measures of Joint Commission Accreditation and Hospital Consumer Assessment of Healthcare Providers and Systems (HCAHPS).

Q4. What is the relationship between the nonprofit hospitals' strategic aggressiveness and financial performance?

H4: There is a reliable relationship between the nonprofit hospitals' strategic aggressiveness and financial performance.

Q5. What is the relationship between nonprofit hospitals' strategic posture and performance measure of the Joint Commission Accreditation?

H5: There is a reliable relationship between nonprofit hospitals' strategic posture and performance measure of the Joint Commission Accreditation.

Q6. What is the relationship between nonprofit hospitals' legitimacy and quality of care performance measure of Joint Commission Accreditation and Hospital Consumer Assessment of Healthcare Providers & Systems (HCAHPS)?

H6: There is a reliable relationship between nonprofit hospitals' legitimacy and quality of care performance measure of Joint Commission Accreditation and Hospital Consumer Assessment of Healthcare Providers & Systems (HCAHPS).

Q7. What is the relationship between nonprofit hospitals' environmental turbulence and strategic posture?

H7: There is a reliable relationship between nonprofit hospitals' environmental turbulence and strategic posture?

CONCEPTUAL AND OPERATIONAL DEFINITIONS

This section provides the conceptual and operational definitions for the independent, intervening, and dependent variables. The independent, intervening, and dependent variables were described to ensure accuracy.

INDEPENDENT VARIABLES

According to Sproul (1995), Independent Variables are defined as "the phenomenon or characteristic hypothesized to be the input variable or presumed cause, which is manipulated and measured (1995). The following summarizes the independent research variables in the study.

HOSPITAL ENVIRONMENTAL TURBULENCE

Conceptual Definition: This is defined as the rapidity of changeability, complexity, familiarity of events, and predictability of the internal and external environments in which the nonprofit hospital operates. Hospital environmental turbulence measured the hospital's response relative to changes in the hospital's internal & external environment (competitors, government organizations, legislative/political changes, economic changes, social/demographic changes, technological changes). The complexity of the hospital's environment is characterized as (a) Speed of change (government policies and regulations) in the hospital industry; (b) Visibility of the future in the environment of the hospital industry; (c) Degree of predictability of patient needs; (d) Complexity of the internal and external environments that affect the hospital.

Environmental Turbulence Sub-Variables

Turbulence Sub-Variables	Code
Complexity	ETC
Familiarity of Events	ETF
Rapidity of Change	ETR
Visibility of the Future	ETV

Table 3

Operational Definition: A healthcare organization's environmental turbulence is defined as the average composite of the nonprofit hospital's environmental turbulence sub-variables as measured on a five-point Likert scales as follows: EVT = (ETC + ETF + ETR + ETV)/4. The environmental turbulence will be measured as the arithmetic mean of the answers from the survey questions: The multiple-choice answers utilized a Likert-type scale of 1 through 5 for turbulence. Some of the survey questions have been adapted from Dr. Lorton's (2006) environmental management strategies survey and Dr. Yousef Ibrahim's (2012) role of multinational companies in sustainable socioeconomic questionnaire. The level of turbulence was determined by the average score of complexity, rapidity of change, visibility of the future, and degree of predictability of the hospital using a 5-point Likert scale.

HOSPITAL STRATEGIC AGGRESSIVENESS

Conceptual Definition: Hospital's strategic aggressiveness is the hospital's past products/services, competitive environments, and marketing strategies and the hospital's response to their environmental turbulence. The hospital's strategic aggressiveness measured the hospital's degree of discontinuity from the past of the hospital's services/ programs, competitive environment, marketing strategies, and the timeliness of introduction of the hospital's new services/programs. The elements contributing to strategic aggressiveness for hospitals are mainly based on the elements of strategic aggressiveness in the Ansoff Strategic Success Model (Ansoff & McDonnell, 1990).

Operational Definition: Lorton (2006) developed questions to measure strategic aggressiveness of Ansoff's theory. The strategic aggressiveness was measured as the arithmetic mean based on the hospital's introduction of new services or technology; their competitive environment and marketing strategies, responsiveness to patients and competition, focus of new services or technology. The mean was calculated by taking the average score of the answers to all the aggressiveness questions based on a Likert scale of 1 to 5. The scale ranged from stable to reactive, anticipatory, entrepreneurial, and creative (Ansoff, McDonnell, 1990).

HOSPITAL CAPABILITY RESPONSIVENESS

Conceptual Definition: Hospital management capability responsiveness is characterized by the ability of management, staff, and the organization to respond to changes in the nonprofit hospital's environment. It is measured through the involvement of management and staff in the climate of the organization, and the competence of the hospital management and staff.

Operational Definition: Hospital capability responsiveness was measured as the arithmetic mean based of the hospital's capability responsiveness of management, staff and the organization to changes in the nonprofit hospital's environment. The scale was based on a 5-point Likert-type scale. The questions will be based on previous researchers' questionnaires measuring a hospital's ability to meet patient needs, management and staff involvement in healthcare issues, the climate of the organization, and the competence of the hospital staff to respond to changes in the environment.

HOSPITAL LEGITIMACY

Conceptual Definition – The combination of the hospital management's ability to achieve their objectives; hospital's organizational culture, management's influence on the organization and analysis of the hospital's impact in the community. The analysis of the hospital management objectives is guided by the governing board and management's ability to achieve their objectives and improve patient's quality of care and health of the community. The hospital's organizational culture is based on the satisfaction level of all the stakeholders (Physicians, nurses, management, staff, and external partners) and participation in the organizational culture. Hospital management's influence on the organization to impact the community. The analysis of the hospitals' role in the community based on their mission and strategy.

Operational Definition – Legitimacy was analyzed by measuring the nonprofit hospital's governing board and management's ability to improve quality of care and their impact on improving the health of the community. Also, legitimacy was measured by analyzing the hospital's organizational culture and their stakeholders' level of satisfaction with the organization. This independent variable was measured using a combination of 12 different questions and taking the average score of all questions and dividing it by the total number of survey questions answered by each hospital. The measurement tool took the average score based on a 5-point Likert-type scale from 1 to 5.

HOSPITAL STRATEGIC POSTURE

Conceptual Definition – The combination of the nonprofit hospital's environmental turbulence, strategic aggressiveness, and capability responsiveness. The strategic posture deals with the nonprofit hospitals engagement and proactive initiatives that extend beyond the organization's operations.

Operational Definition – Measured by calculating the arithmetic mean for the environmental turbulence, strategic aggressiveness and capability responsiveness questions: (Q2 +Q3+Q4+Q5+Q6+Q7+Q8+Q9+Q10+Q11+Q12+Q13+Q14+Q1 5+Q16+Q17)/16

INTERVENING VARIABLES

Two intervening variables—hospital aggressiveness and hospital capability responsiveness—was calculated as "gaps" or differences between hospital environmental turbulence and the two respective independent variables. These gaps are identified as the strategic aggressiveness gap and the capability responsiveness gap.

HOSPITAL STRATEGIC AGGRESSIVENESS GAP

Conceptual definition – The strategic aggressiveness gap represents the extent to which the hospital's aggressiveness differs from the environmental turbulence. A small gap indicates a good alignment between strategic aggressiveness and environmental turbulence.

Operational definition – The strategic aggressiveness gap is measured as the absolute difference between the scores of the strategic aggressiveness and the environmental turbulence for each respondent.

The value is based on the 5-point numerical scales of the strategic aggressiveness and the environmental turbulence but yields scores in which the possible range is 1 to 5.

HOSPITAL CAPABILITY RESPONSIVENESS GAP

Conceptual definition – The capability responsiveness gap represents the extent to which the hospital responsiveness differs from the environmental turbulence. A small gap indicates a good alignment between capability responsiveness and the environmental turbulence.

Operational definition – The capability responsiveness gap is measured as the absolute difference between the scores of the capability responsiveness and the environmental turbulence for each respondent. The value is based on the 5-point numerical scales of the capability responsiveness and the environmental turbulence but yields scores in which the possible range is 1 to 5.

DEPENDENT VARIABLE

Hospital performance is the dependent variable. Nonprofit hospital performance was measured using the Joint Commission's accreditation status, the hospital consumer assessment of healthcare provider survey (HCAHPS), and financial performance of nonprofit hospitals.

NONPROFIT HOSPITAL PERFORMANCE MEASURES

The performance measures are based on the Joint Commission Accreditation status and quality measures. Also, the Hospital Consumer Assessment of Healthcare Providers & Systems and financial performance of the nonprofit hospitals.

JOINT COMMISSION ACCREDITATION OF HEALTHCARE ORGANIZATIONS

Conceptual definition – The Joint Commission's accreditation of a hospital is a widely recognized national standard for evaluating and demonstrating high quality of care services for hospitals. The Joint commission accreditation is a set of standards that focus on patient safety and quality of care provided by healthcare organizations (https://www.jointcommission.org/assets/1/18/171110_Accreditation_Guide_Hospitals_FINAL.pdf).

Operational definition – The Joint Commission's accreditation was obtained from the Joint Commission's website and scored based on the average scores of the nonprofit hospital's accreditations status over the past five years from 2013 to 2017.

The Joint Commission's scores was based on the hospital's initial accreditation scores of 5 – Accredited, 4 – Accredited with follow-up survey, 3 - Preliminary denial of accreditation, 2 – Denial of accreditation, 1 – Did not participate in Joint Commission's accreditation.

The JCAHO accreditation status are listed in Table 4.

Likert Scale	Accreditation Status
5	Accredited with Gold Seal
4	Accredited with follow up survey
3	Partially Accredited
2	Accreditation Denied
1	Did not participate in JCAHO survey

Table 4

HOSPITAL CONSUMER ASSESSMENT OF HEALTHCARE

PROVIDERS AND SYSTEMS (HCAHPS)

Conceptual definition - The Hospital Consumer Assessment of Healthcare Providers and Systems is a standardized, publicly reported survey of patients' perspective of hospital care. It is data collection methodology that has been in use since 2006 to measure patients' perspectives of hospital care. It is a 32-item survey instrument and data collection methodology for measuring patients' perception of their hospital care that's designed to produce comparable data on the patient's perspective on care that allows objective and meaningful comparisons between hospitals.

The seven composites summarized how well nurses and doctors communicate with patients, how well the staff communicates with patients about medicines, whether key information is provided at discharge, and how well patients understand the type of care they need after leaving the hospital.

Two of the HCAHPS individual items address the cleanliness and quiet of patients' rooms while the two global items capture patients overall rating of the hospital and whether they would recommend the hospital to family and friends. HCAHPS scores are designed for use at the hospital level for the comparison of hospitals to each other. Official HCAHPS scores are based on four consecutive quarters of patient surveys publicly reported on the Hospital Compare website at https://www.medicare. gove/hospitalcompare.

Operational definition – Hospital Consumer Assessment of Healthcare Providers and Systems (HCAHPS) was measured by taking the final average summary star rating score of the 9 elements of the HCAHPS measures for each year the hospital participated in the HCAHPS Survey. The HCAHPS survey contains 32 perspectives on care and patient rating items that encompass eleven key topics:

Communication with doctors, communication with nurses, responsiveness of hospital staff, pain management, communication about medicines, discharge information, cleanliness of the hospital environment, quietness of the hospital environment, and transition of care, hospital rating and recommendation of the hospital (www.hcahpsonline.org).

HCAHPS star ratings are applied to each of the 11 publicly reported HCAHPS measures. The star rating for each of the 11 HCAHPS measures is determined by applying a clustering algorithm to the individual measure scores. The summary star rating is the average of all the star ratings of the HCAHPS measures and constructed from the following components. The Star Ratings from each of the 11 HCAHPS Composite Measures. Communication with Nurses, Communication with Doctors, Responsiveness of Hospital Staff, Pain Management, Communication about Medicines, Discharge Information, and Care Transition. A single Star Rating for the HCAHPS Individual Items. The average of the Star Ratings assigned to Cleanliness of Hospital Environment and Quietness of Hospital Environment. A single Star Rating for the HCAHPS Global Items. The average of the Star Ratings assigned to Hospital Rating and recommendations of the Hospital.

The final average HCAHPS Summary Star Rating score was measured based on a Likert-Scale of 1 to 5 stars for each year the hospital participated in the HCAHPS Survey from 2013 to 2017. The summary 5-star rating scale was based on the final score average for each nonprofit hospital.

4-5 – stars – Top Performers

3-4 – Above Average Performers

2-3 – Average Performers

1-2 – Below Average Performers

1 – Did not participate in the HCAHPS Survey

The HCAHPS status are listed in Table 5.

HCAHPS Star Rating score	Rating interpretation
4 - 5	Top Performers
3 - 4	Above Average Performers
2 - 3	Average Performers
1 - 2	Below Average Performers
1	Did not participate

Table 5

NONPROFIT HOSPITAL FINANCIAL PERFORMANCE

Conceptual definition is the financial performance measures of nonprofit hospitals based on their operating margin, total margin, return on equity, return on assets, and cash flow margin.

Operating margin is net operating income divided by total revenue.

Total margin is excess revenues over expenses (Net income) divided by total revenue multiplied by 100.

Return on equity (ROE) is the amount of net income or excess of revenues over expenses earned per dollar of equity investment.

Return on assets (ROA) is an indicator of how profitable the organization is relative to its assets. ROA is net income divided by total assets.

Cash Flow Margin is an important profitability ratio that shows cash flow from operating activities over net revenue. The ratio is calculated by dividing the operating cash flow of the hospital sales.

Operational definition – Financial performance on nonprofit hospitals is based on the hospital's operating margin, total margin, return on equity, return on assets, and cash flow margin. This was measured based on each hospital's margins compared to other hospitals. Different measurement tools was used to help with determining the healthcare organizations' overall performance. The financial performance measurement tool utilized was the nonprofit hospital's financial performance.

Nonprofit Hospital Financial Performance Table

Financial Performance Measures	Determinants	Formula
Operating Margin (OM)	(Total operating revenue – Total operating expense)/ Total Operating Revenue (TOR)	= (TOR – TOE)/TOR
Total Margin ™	(Total Operating revenue/ Total Operating expenses) X 100	= NI/TR X 100
Return on Equity (ROE)	Net Income/(Total Assets – Total liabilities) X 100	= NI/(TA – TL) X 100
Return on Assets (ROA)	Net Income/Total Assets X 100	= NI/TA X 100
Cash Flow Margin (CFM)	Net income + interest+Depreciation/ Total revenue	NI+Int+Depreciation/ TR

Table 6

These performance measures was gathered from the Joint Commission's website and hospital administrators. The Joint Commission's website provides public access to view and download hospital's Joint Commission results for accreditation. The Hospital Consumer Assessment of Healthcare Providers and Systems provides the summary rating scores for all hospitals that participated in the survey. The financial statement information was gathered from different healthcare websites such as the American Hospital Directory (https://www.ahd.com) and individual hospital websites.

CHAPTER 2B SUMMARY

Chapter 2B presented the literature review, research questions, hypotheses, and variable definitions pertaining to the research model of this study. The conceptual and operational definitions of the variables were given, along with the strategic management framework for the research. This chapter also contained a discussion of research on the strategic success model factors, legitimacy strategies, and organizational strategies of nonprofit and federal hospitals. In addition, it compared their relationship to performance in nonprofit hospitals.

RESEARCH METHODOLOGY

*C*hapter 3 describes the research strategy, research population, sampling methodology, research instrumentation, research sample, validity and reliability, and data analysis methodology used to evaluate the hypotheses identified in Chapter 2. Assumptions and probable limitations in reliability and validity, and delimitation are then summarized followed by the chapter summary.

The purpose of this section was to investigate the relationship between Dr. Igor Ansoff's strategic success factors (environmental turbulence, strategic aggressiveness, and capability responsiveness) and the performance measures of nonprofit hospitals in the United States. This section evaluates the impact of environmental turbulence, strategic aggressiveness, capability responsiveness and social factors (legitimacy) on the performance measures of nonprofit hospitals.

RESEARCH STRATEGY

The research strategy performs a descriptive and correlational study aimed to determine the relationship between the multiple variables. The descriptive and correlational study involved the following methods: The topic facts, variables, and characteristics were described. A survey instrument was developed capable of acquiring appropriate data and designed for validity and reliability. The survey instrument solicited both demographic data and research data. The survey instrument's research questions used a 5-point Likert scale and was constructed to acquire real setting data based on past and current data. The survey instrument was tested for validity and reliability.

A pilot test of the survey instrument was conducted with two Nonprofit hospital executives to check for understandability, time required, and appropriateness of the survey questions. The pilot test survey instruments were not used as part of the research database. A research target organization list was developed. Surveys involving hospital executives or staff from the cross-sectional representation sample of the research target organization list was conducted requesting their participation.

The survey instrument was provided to those nonprofit hospital executives or staff agreeing to participate in the study. The primary data was received from the participating nonprofit hospital executives or staff, who completed the provided survey instrument. The survey instrument's data was entered into the research Database Qualtrics. Statistical analyses were performed to correlate relationships between independent and dependent variables. Collecting and analyzing the variables specified in the research problem.

The study required a systematic method that would be effective and accurate in describing the relationship among the variables measured. It was therefore, designed and conducted as a descriptive, correlational research. The variables of this study consisted of five independent variables, three dependent variables and two intervening variables. The study utilized both primary and secondary data to determine the relationship between Ansoff's strategic success factors (Environmental turbulence, strategic aggressiveness, and capability responsiveness), along with legitimacy and nonprofit hospital performance measures.

The data analyses utilized Spearman's rho correlation and linear regression to determine the statistical significance between the independent variables and the dependent variables. The dependent variable was categorized by quality performance measures of Joint Commission Accreditation scores, Hospital Consumer Assessment of Healthcare Providers and Systems Scores, and financial performance measures (Operating margin, Total margin, Return on Equity, Return on Assets, and Cash flow margin) was assessed. The independent variables are environmental turbulence, hospital aggressiveness, capability responsiveness, legitimacy, and strategic posture. The intervening variables are the hospital aggressiveness gap and the hospital capability responsiveness gap; the dependent variable is performances (JCAHO Scores, HCAHPS scores, Financial data).

All variable items are measured on a 5-point Likert scale. The data for each variable will be evaluated as interval scales. The researcher collected archival data from the Joint Commission's website, Hospital Compare, and the American Hospital Directory website to gather Joint Commission Accreditation scores, Hospital Consumer Assessment of Healthcare Providers and Systems Scores, and the American Hospital Directory to collect the financial performance of participating nonprofit hospitals. The data range is for five-year study period from 2013 to 2017.

A gap in the alignment between environmental turbulence, aggressiveness, and responsiveness was measured as the hospital strategic aggressiveness gap and capability responsiveness gap. The methodology used for this study was derived from the strategic success model presented by Ansoff and McDonnell (1990).

RESEARCH POPULATION

The research population was represented by the almost 4,000 nonprofit hospitals in the United States. The research population was derived from the American Hospital Association's (AHA) 2017 Hospital Directory database. The targeted hospitals were the federal, state, local and other community nonprofit hospitals in the United States with more than one bed. The AHA maintains a listing of all nonprofit federal, state, local, health hospitals including teaching hospitals. The hospitals excluded from the research was Psychiatric or Behavioral hospitals, Public Health Services, Native American hospitals, U.S. Military and Veteran Administration Hospitals.

SAMPLE METHODOLOGY

The following methodology was used to generate the research sample: 1. The American Hospital Association's 2017 Directory Database listing of nonprofit hospitals was used to identify nonprofit hospitals. The database was used as reference from which to select a simple random selection of hospitals for the study. The data can be accessed from the internet at the American Hospital Association website at https://www.ahd.com. A 2017 listing of all nonprofit hospitals were obtained from the American Hospital Association. More than 3,900 hospitals fit the criteria for the study.

A simple random sample of the hospitals was done using Microsoft Excel. The listing of hospitals was placed into an Excel spreadsheet and a simple random sample selection process to determine the first 1,000 federal, state, local, other nonprofit hospitals for the study. All the information was available to use as potential primary data sources. The selection criteria limited potential participants based on hospital type.

The samples for this study were collected by first extracting the available data for 3,900 nonprofit hospitals from the American Hospital Association directory. The data was inputted into Microsoft Excel program, and all even numbered hospitals was selected. Over 1,054 nonprofit hospitals were selected, and letters mailed to the hospital administrators. After 30 days, another 526 hospitals were contacted via phone call, email, Facebook, and hospital websites requesting their participation in the survey. A total of 1,054 hospitals had letters mailed to them and another 526 nonprofit hospitals were called or sent messages via Facebook or via their hospital websites.

The survey questionnaire was imported into the Qualtrics program. A cover letter was created and imported into Qualtrics for the hospital executives or staff to read prior to participating in the study. Also, a copy of the cover letter was mailed to them to complete the survey, which contained a description of the purpose of the study, and the link for completing the survey online. The cover letter includes an e-mail address to request a summary report of the research. The cover letter and survey is included in Appendix A. Approximately 1,054 cover letters were mailed to the first 1,054 hospitals in the simple random sample list of federal, state, local and other community nonprofit hospitals throughout the United States. Another 526 nonprofit community hospitals were contacted via email, Facebook or hospital websites. Data analysis was concluded 8 weeks after the final surveys were completed. To obtain the qualitative data, the researcher collected the performance measures on accreditation status, Hospital Consumer Assessment of Healthcare Providers and Systems Survey ratings and financial information from the Joint Commission, Hospital Compare and the American Hospital Directory websites. A total of 43 nonprofit hospitals completed the survey. The distribution of hospitals were as follows: 13 – Other, nonprofit hospitals; 15 – Local government nonprofit hospitals; 6 - Public community nonprofit hospitals; 2 – State, nonprofit hospitals; 7 – Teaching nonprofit hospitals.

SURVEY INSTRUMENT

Qualtrics online survey site was used to post the survey instrument for data collection (see Appendix A). The survey designated "The Relationship Between Strategic Success Paradigm and Performance of Nonprofit Hospitals" was distributed utilizing a cover letter that was sent to the Administration Department at nonprofit hospitals across the United States.

All respondents received a guarantee anonymity and an explanation of the participant's bill of rights and the Informed Consent Agreement prior to initiation of the online survey (see Appendix A). Respondents of the survey were provided a copy of the cover letter via mail and directed to the survey online prior to site entry describing the purpose of the study and explaining the participant's bill of rights.

All respondents were offered a "Summary of the Survey Results and Conclusions" by email or mail to protect the anonymity of the survey itself.

The research was constructed to have the minimal risk to all participants. The questionnaire was constructed to maintain the respondent's anonymity, since no individual or hospital names were solicited or received.

RESEARCH DATA COLLECTION METHODOLOGY

The research data was to be derived from completed survey instruments from hospital executives (i.e. CEOs, CFOs, COOs, Directors, Managers) or hospital staff (physicians, technicians, or administrative personnel) extracted from the target research sample database. The data collection process followed these steps:

A pilot sample was conducted by soliciting one nonprofit hospital manager from one of the nonprofit hospitals in California to complete the survey instrument. After the data was collected, follow-up questions were asked regarding the instrument's understandability, validity and quality. The nonprofit hospital manager found the survey instrument to be understandable and of high quality. The data from the pilot survey was used in the research database. The nonprofit hospital manager was contacted via email and agreed to participate in completing the survey instrument.

SAMPLING FRAME

The sampling frame was taken from the American Hospital Association Directory of government, state, local, and other nonprofit acute care hospitals in the United States. The target population from the American Hospital Association Directory of government, state, local or other nonprofit acute care hospitals were hospital administrators or executives or management. A cover page describing the research survey's purpose, time required, importance, and confidentiality of the data was stated. If the executive staff or administrative staff agreed to participate in the survey.

SAMPLE SIZE

The target population was comprised of Nonprofit government, state local and other acute and critical care hospitals. The target population consisted of 3,909 hospitals from all 50 states plus the District of Columbia. The final sample size was comprised of 1,580 nonprofit hospitals that reported financial, Joint Commission Accreditation, and Hospital Consumer Assessment of Healthcare Providers and Systems Survey ratings data for five consecutive years from 2013 to 2017. The sample size for the research study was 43 nonprofit hospitals.

RESEARCH INSTRUMENTATION

The survey instrument was developed capable of acquiring all appropriate data and designed for validity and reliability. The survey instrument used the following to obtain or assign numerical values for the various variables. 5-point Likert scale;

Average of multiple sub-variables; Actual raw data value provided by survey respondent on a survey instrument.

The survey instrument did not request hospital demographic data to keep the survey instrument anonymous. The approved survey instrument is in Appendix A. The means used for collecting data was a survey adapted from the Ansoff model for diagnosing the level of environmental turbulence, strategic aggressiveness and capability responsiveness. Another set of questions was utilized for diagnosing legitimacy and strategic posture.

DATA ANALYSIS

This study used two statistical tests to analyze the data. The following are the methods employed:

1. Spearman r correlations were used to test the hypothesis of the degree of association between variables.
2. Linear regression was utilized to analyze the effects of the independent and dependent variable.

INDEPENDENT VARIABLES

The variables measured by the survey questionnaire were hospital environmental turbulence, hospital aggressiveness, hospital capability responsiveness, hospital legitimacy.

The questions were grouped on the survey to assess each variable, but this was not indicated to respondents. Each variable had multiple questions.

SURVEY QUESTIONS

SURVEY QUESTIONS FOR HOSPITAL ENVIRONMENTAL TURBULENCE

Calculation: (Q2 + Q3 + Q4 + Q5)/4

Questions 2 through 5 addressed the following various aspects of environmental turbulence with respect to nonprofit hospitals.

- Question 2 – The complexity of changes which occurred in the environment of the hospital.
- Question 3 – The familiarity of changes, which occurred in the hospital's environment.
- Question 4 – Speed of change in the hospital's environment.
- Question 5 – The visibility of the future in the environment

The hospital's turbulence level was calculated through averaging the scores on a Likert scale of 1 – 5 for a series of questions: where 1 means changes are rare or slow and we don't worry about change; 2 means when changes come, we usually react easily to them; 3 means when changes come, we normally react in time; 4 means when changes occur, we are usually trying to catch up with them; and 5 means changes are extremely fast and chaotic, and we struggle to keep up with them. The scores for questions 2 through 5 were averaged and the answer was divided by 4.

SURVEY QUESTIONS FOR HOSPITAL STRATEGIC AGGRESSIVENESS

Calculation: (Q6 + Q7 + Q8 + Q9 + Q10 + Q11 + Q12)/7

Questions 6 through 12 addressed the following various aspects of hospital's strategic aggressiveness.

- Question 6 – How often has the hospital introduced new healthcare services?
- Question 7 – To what extent have the hospital implemented new healthcare technology?
- Question 8 - How would you describe the hospital among its competitors in hospital performance measures (financial)?
- Question 9 – How would you describe the hospital among its competitors in performance measures (Joint Commission Accreditation)?
- Question 10 – How would you describe the hospital among its competitors in hospital performance measure in patient satisfaction (HCAHPS)?
- Question 11 – How would you characterize management's strategy on the hospital/health system performance (financial, Joint Commission Accreditation, and HCAHPS scores)?
- Question 12 – What is your hospital/health system strategy for interacting with the regulatory agencies?

Survey respondents rated each aspect of hospital strategy aggressiveness based on the five choices for each question.

The scores for possible answers to each question ranged from 1 to 5. If a question was not answered, the score was based on the average remaining questions.

SURVEY QUESTIONS FOR HOSPITAL CAPABILITY RESPONSIVENESS

Calculation: (Q13 + Q14 + Q15 + Q16 + Q17 + Q18)/6

Questions 13 through 18 addressed the various aspects of hospital capability responsiveness.

- Question 13– How would you describe management's ability to respond to changes in the environment?
- Question 14 – How would you describe the staff's ability to respond to changes in the environment?
- Question 15 – What has been your hospital/health system's attitude toward implementing new healthcare technology?
- Question 16 – How often did the hospital/health system governing board assist in improving quality of care?
- Question 17 – How often did management assist in improving quality of care?
- Question 18 – How would you rate your hospital/health system expansion of its patient services?

Survey respondents rated each aspect of hospital capability responsiveness based on the five choices for each question. The scores for possible answers to each question ranged from

1 to 5. If a question was not answered, the scores were based on the average remaining questions.

SURVEY QUESTIONS FOR LEGITIMACY

Calculation: (Q19 + Q20 + Q21 + Q22 + Q23 + Q24 + Q25 + Q26 + 27)/9

Questions 19 through 26 addressed the various aspects of hospital legitimacy.

- Question 19 – How would you rate your hospital/health system's community benefits programs (initiatives and activities to improve health in the community) against other nonprofit hospitals/health systems across the country?
- Question 20 – How did your hospital/health system community programs (initiatives and activities to improve health in the community) influence the hospital/health system's financial performance?
- Question 21 – How did your hospital/health system community programs (initiatives and activities to improve health in the community) influence the hospital/health system's patient satisfaction (HCAHPS)?
- Question 22 – How did your hospital/health system rate the influence on federal/state agencies (such influence on JCAHO, OSHA, American Hospital Association, American Medical Association, etc...) on the hospital/health system Joint Commission Accreditation scores?

- Question 23 – How would you rate the physician satisfaction in your hospital/health system?
- Question 24 – How would you rate the nurse work satisfaction in your hospital/health system?
- Question 25 – How would you rate management's (management staff) level of satisfaction in your hospital?
- Question 26 – How would you rate external stakeholders (Suppliers, partnerships with physician groups, community, etc…) level of satisfaction with your hospital/ health system?
- Question 27 – How would you rate hospital/health system employees (technicians, ancillary staff, and other staff) level of satisfaction with your hospital/health system?

Survey respondents rated each aspect of hospital Legitimacy based on the five choices for each question. The scores for possible answers to each question ranged from 1 to 5. If a question was not answered, the scores were based on the average remaining questions.

SURVEY QUESTIONS FOR NONPROFIT HOSPITAL PERFORMANCE MEASURES

Questions 28 through 34 addressed the Nonprofit Hospital's performance measures based on hospital/health system patient satisfaction (HCAHPS) scores, Joint Commission Accreditation of Health Care Organizations (JCAHO) scores and financial performance.

- Question 28 – Please indicate your hospital or healthcare organization's average score on their Joint Commission Accreditation on Healthcare Organizations over the past five years?
- Question 29 – Please indicate your hospital or healthcare organization's average Hospital Consumer Assessment of Healthcare Providers and Systems (HCAHPS) average rating score over the past five years?
- Question 30 – Please provide your hospital's operating margin average over the past 5 years.
- Question 31 – Please provide your hospital's total margin average over the past 5 years.
- Question 32 – Please provide your hospital's Return on Assets (ROA) average over the past 5 years.
- Question 33 – Please provide your hospital's Return on Equity (ROE) average over the past 5 years.
- Question 34 – Please provide your hospital's Cash Flow Margin average over the past 5 years?

INTERVENING VARIABLES

HOSPITAL STRATEGY AGGRESSIVENESS GAP

Calculations: (Hospital environmental turbulence + hospital strategy aggressiveness). The hospital strategy aggressiveness gap was an intervening variable with scores ranging from 1 to 5. It measured the alignment between hospital environmental turbulence and strategy aggressiveness. The hospital strategy aggressiveness gap was calculated by taking the absolute value of the difference between the hospital's strategy aggressiveness and the environmental turbulence.

HOSPITAL CAPABILITY RESPONSIVENESS GAP

Calculation: (Hospital environmental turbulence – hospital capability responsiveness) ranging from 1 to 5. It measured the alignment between hospital environmental turbulence and capability responsiveness. The hospital capability responsiveness gap was calculated by taking the absolute value of the difference between the hospital capability responsiveness and environmental turbulence.

DEPENDENT VARIABLES

The dependent variables are the hospital Joint Commission on Accreditation of Healthcare Organizations (JCAHO) scores, the hospital Consumer Assessment of Healthcare Providers and Systems (HCAPHS) scores and financial performance (Operating margin, Total margin, Return on Equity, Return on Assets, and cash flow margin).

HOSPITAL JOINT COMMISSION ACCREDITATION SCORE

The hospital quality of care score was measured using hospital's Joint Commission on Accreditation of Healthcare Organizations (JCAHO) scores. These scores measure the hospital's quality of care ranging from 1 to 5. The Joint Commission on Accreditation of Healthcare Organizations categories are as follows: 1 – Did not participate in Accreditation; 2 – Prepared but denied accreditation; 3 – Preliminary denied accreditation, but then accredited; 4 – Accredited with follow-up survey, but then accredited; 5 – Fully accredited with a Gold Seal.

The Joint Commission on Accreditation of Healthcare Organizations was measured by averaging the scores for each hospital JCAHO scores over the past five years taken from the American Hospital Directory website.

HOSPITAL CONSUMER ASSESSMENT OF HEALTHCARE PROVIDERS & SYSTEMS (HCAHPS) SCORE

The hospital patient satisfaction scores was measured using the Hospital Consumer Assessment of Healthcare Providers and Systems (HCAHPS) scores. These scores measure the patient's perspective of care and satisfaction. The HCAHPS scores range is did not participate in HCAHPS; 1 to 2 Stars Rating; 2 to 3 Star Rating; 3 to 4 Star Rating; 4 to 5 Star Rating. The value of the HCAHPS scores was calculated by averaging the HCAHPS scores for each hospital over the past five years. This data was gathered from the Centers for Medicare and Medicaid Services (CMS) hospital compare website at https://www.medicare.gov/HospitalCompare/search.html.

HOSPITAL FINANCIAL PERFORMANCE

The hospital financial performance was measured using each hospital's (operating margin, total margin, return on equity, return on assets, and cash flow margin) financial performance measures to determine overall financial performance.

Each hospital's financial performance included the hospital's operating margin, total margin, return on equity, return on assets, and cash flow margin to determine their financial viability. The financial status was calculated to determine financial viability. The financial statements of the hospitals was extracted from the American Hospital Directory at https://www.ahd.com over a five years span from 2013 to 2017 and averaged.

Table 6.1. Formulas of Financial Performance Indicators

operating margin, total margin, return on equity, return on assets, and cash flow margin

Financial Performance (DV) Indicators	Formulas
1. Operating Margin (OM)	= (Operating Income)/(Total Operating Revenue) Where, Operating Income = Total Operating Revenue – Total Operating Expense
2. Total Margin	= Total Profit Margin – Operating Profit Margin = [(Net Income)/(Total Revenue)]- [(Operating Income)/(Total Operating Revenue)] Where, Total Revenue = Total Patient Revenue + Total Non-Patient Revenue
3. Return on Assets	= (Net Income)/(Total Assets)
4. Return on Equity	= (Net Income)/(Total Equity)
5. Cash Flow Margin	= (Operating Income + Depreciation Expense + Interest Expense)/(Net Patient Revenue) Where Net Patient Revenue = Total Patient Revenue – Contractual Allowances (Discounts)

VALIDITY AND RELIABILITY

The data elements for the survey questionnaire were selected by the researcher, based on extensive literature review and professional experience gained over 20 years of healthcare industry experience. The validity of the survey questionnaire was verified by using a pilot survey on a nonprofit hospital executive from one of California nonprofit hospitals, who completed the questionnaire and found all questions valid and reliable to the study. Also, using the proven Joint Commission Accreditation for measuring healthcare quality of care in healthcare organizations and the HCAHPS Survey for measuring patient satisfaction. Health systems and hospitals financial performance information was gathered from the American Hospital Directory website.

All variables was measured by multiple questions. Reliability of the variables was measured using the coefficient alpha (Cronbach's alpha). It should be noted that the hospital's strategic aggressiveness, capability responsiveness, legitimacy and the performance measures are both complex, multidimensional variables that represent the sum of varied elements to produce scores.

DATA ANALYSIS

The information received from Qualtrics results was saved in an excel spreadsheet and transferred to an SPSS data file. Further analysis included calculating the hospital strategic aggressiveness gap and capability responsiveness gap based on the nonprofit hospitals' turbulence level and corresponding strategic aggressiveness and capability responsiveness. The data sets were from 43 Nonprofit Community hospitals over with the performance measures of Joint Commission Accreditation, Hospital Consumer Assessment of Healthcare Providers & Systems, and financial information over five consecutive years from 2013 to 2017.

Data analyses for this study consisted of examining archival Joint Commission Accreditation and HCAHPS data and financial data that were self-reported to the American Hospital Directory (AHD) at https://www.ahd.com and Centers for Medicare & Medicaid (CMS) on the Medicare website at https://www.medicare.gov/hospitalcompare.search.html? Given the complexity of the data, quantitative analyses encompassed both descriptive and inferential statistical techniques that were relevant and appropriate for the all the data. SPSS were used to perform descriptive and inferential statistical analyses.

DESCRIPTIVE STATISTICS

Different descriptive statistics were used to analyze the data for this study. These statistics included measuring the mean and median, variances and standard deviation.

A Spearman correlation was run to test each hypothesis with an independent and dependent variable. This study used a percent value as the statistical significance ($p < .05$). Spearman

(r) was calculated to test the research hypotheses seeking degrees of correlation.

INFERENTIAL STATISTICS

The inferential statistics was evaluated to analyze the archival data and a linear regression was performed to test frequency distribution of the categorical variables measuring nonprofit hospital performance (Joint Commission Accreditation, HCAHPS scores, and financial information). The independent variables of strategic aggressiveness, capability responsiveness, environmental turbulence, legitimacy, and strategic posture were analyzed using linear regression. Statistically significant results from the linear regression tests were compared for strategic aggressiveness, capability responsiveness, legitimacy using linear regression. Testing of Hypothesis 1 was conducted using Spearman (r). The nonprofit hospital's financial performance measure was regressed based on the hospitals' strategic aggressiveness gap.

Testing of Hypothesis 2 was conducted using Spearman (r) to determine significance between the nonprofit hospitals' capability responsiveness gap and the performance measure of quality performance measures Joint Commission Accreditation and Hospital Consumer Assessment of Healthcare Providers & Systems (HCAHPS).

Testing of Hypothesis 3 was conducted using Spearman (r) to determine, if there was statistical significance between the variables; capability responsiveness and the performance measures – Joint Commission Accreditation and Hospital Consumer Assessment of Healthcare Providers & Systems (HCAHPS).

Testing of Hypothesis 4 was conducted using Spearman (r) to determine, if there was statistical significance between the variables; strategic aggressiveness and financial performance measure.

Testing of Hypothesis 5 was conducted using Spearman (r) to determine, if there was statistical significance between the variables; Strategic Posture and the performance measures of the Joint Commission Accreditation and HCAHPS. Testing of Hypothesis 6 was conducted using Spearman (r) to determine, if there was statistical significance between the variables; legitimacy and quality performance measures Joint Commission Accreditation and HCAHPS. Testing of Hypothesis 7 was conducted using Spearman (r) to determine, if there was statistical significance between the variables; environmental turbulence and strategic posture.

DATA ASSUMPTIONS

A minimum of 100 survey instruments were expected to be completed and received by the researcher. The likelihood of getting 100 completed surveys was thought to be reasonable based on the researcher's membership and support from the American College of Healthcare Executives Association, American Hospital Association and Linkedin social network.

It was assumed that (a) at least 100 participants would agree to complete the survey, and that (b) the completed survey instruments would be returned by at least 5% of the nonprofit hospital executives or staff, who agreed to participate in the survey. Only 43 out of the 1,580 nonprofit hospitals agreed to participate in the study.

1. The survey participants were qualified, understood each question, took an appropriate amount of time to think about the questions' response alternatives, and answered truthfully to the best of their knowledge.
2. The survey participants had appropriate knowledge regarding the various questions and responded accurately.
3. The referenced research of others is valid. Their research was used as a foundation for this study's research.
4. The data collection and analysis methods used are valid and appropriate for this study.

LIMITATIONS

The following are limitations of the research methodology: The study was limited to U.S. nonprofit government, state, local government, and other hospitals. For profit hospitals and hospitals outside of the United States may provide different results. The small number of completed survey instruments does not reflect the total population. The population that did not respond may affect the research variables differently than those participating in the survey.

CHAPTER SUMMARY

Chapter 3 has identified the research strategy, research population, sampling methodology, research instrumentation, survey, research sample, method for establishing validity, method for establishing reliability, and data analysis methodology that was used to evaluate the hypotheses identified in Chapter 2.

RESEARCH QUESTIONS AND RESEARCH HYPOTHESES

Research Question	Research Hypothesis
Q1. What is the relationship between the nonprofits' strategic aggressiveness gap and financial performance	**H1.** There is a reliable relationship between the nonprofit hospitals' strategic aggressiveness gap and financial performance.
Q2. What is the relationship between nonprofit hospital capability responsiveness gap and performance?	**H2.** There is a relationship between the nonprofit hospitals' capability responsiveness gap and performance.
Q3. What is the relationship between nonprofit hospitals' capability responsiveness and financial performance?	**H3.** There is a reliable relationship between nonprofit hospitals' capability responsiveness and financial performance.
Q4. What is the relationship between nonprofit hospitals' strategic aggressiveness and financial performance?	**H4.** There is a reliable relationship between nonprofit hospitals' strategic aggressiveness and financial performance.
Q5. What is the relationship between nonprofit hospitals' strategy posture and performance?	**Q5.** There is a relationship between nonprofit hospitals' strategic posture and performance.
Q6. What is the relationship between legitimacy and Performance?	**Q6.** There is a reliable relationship between legitimacy and performance.
Q7. What is the relationship between hospitals' environmental turbulence and strategic posture?	**Q7.** There is a reliable relationship between hospitals' environmental turbulence and strategic posture.

Table 7

SUMMARY OF STATISTICAL TESTS

Research Hypothesis	Null Hypothesis	Statistical Test
H1. There is a reliable relationship between the nonprofit hospitals' strategic aggressiveness gap and financial performance.	**H1.** There is no reliable relationship between the nonprofit hospitals' strategic aggressiveness gap and financial performance.	Correlation (Spearman's rho)
H2. There is a reliable relationship between the nonprofit hospitals' capability responsiveness gap and quality performance measures of Joint Commission Accreditation and HCAHPS.	**H2.** There is no reliable relationship between the nonprofit hospitals' capability responsiveness gap and quality performance measures of Joint Commission Accreditation and HCAHPS.	Correlation (Spearman's rho)
H3. There is a reliable relationship between the nonprofit hospitals' capability responsiveness and quality performance measures of Joint Commission Accreditation and HCAHPS.	**H3.** There is no reliable relationship between the nonprofit hospitals' capability responsiveness and quality performance measures of Joint Commission Accreditation and HCAHPS.	Correlation (Spearman's rho)
H4. There is a reliable relationship between the nonprofit hospitals' strategic aggressiveness and financial performance.	**H4.** There is no reliable relationship between the nonprofit hospitals' strategic aggressiveness and financial performance.	Correlation (Spearman's rho)
Q5. There is a reliable relationship between the nonprofit hospitals' strategic posture and performance measure of the Joint Commission Accreditation.	**Q5.** There is no reliable relationship between the nonprofit hospitals' strategic posture and performance measure of the Joint Commission Accreditation.	Correlation (Spearman's rho)
Q6. There is a reliable relationship between the nonprofit hospitals' legitimacy and quality performance measures of the Joint Commission Accreditation and HCAHPS.	**Q6.** There is no reliable relationship between the nonprofit hospitals' legitimacy and quality performance measures of the Joint Commission Accreditation and HCAHPS.	Correlation (Spearman's rho)
Q7. There is a reliable relationship between the nonprofit hospitals' environmental turbulence and strategic posture.	**Q7.** There is no reliable relationship between the nonprofit hospitals' environmental turbulence and strategic posture.	Correlation (Spearman's rho)

Table 8

CHAPTER 4

RESEARCH FINDINGS

$\mathcal{T}$his chapter presents the research study's findings by presenting the results of the data analysis of the seven hypotheses, results of additional findings, and an overall summary of the survey information collected. The research study was designed to investigate the relationship between nonprofit hospitals' environmental factors, strategic behavior, legitimacy, strategic posture and their performance measures of the Joint Commission Accreditation, Hospital Consumer Assessment of Healthcare Providers and Systems (HCAHPS).

The study analyzed nonprofit hospitals' environmental turbulence levels, strategic aggressiveness, capability responsiveness and the impact on the nonprofit hospitals' performance measures.

Also, the study reviewed the nonprofit hospitals' legitimacy and strategic posture to determine the impact on the nonprofit hospitals' performance. In this study, the independent variables environmental turbulence, strategic aggressiveness and capability responsiveness encompassed ten different measures in the survey questionnaire designed to provide the strategic behavior of nonprofit hospitals. The other moderating variables of strategic posture and legitimacy was measured by several survey questions designed to provide the strategic posture and legitimacy of the nonprofit hospitals and their impact on the nonprofit hospital's performance measures. The dependent variable of hospital performance was indicated by three performance measurement categories: Joint Commission Accreditation status, Hospital Consumer Assessment of Healthcare Providers and Systems (HCAHPS) star rating score, and financial performance. The dependent variable of financial performance was measured by five indicators: operating margin, total margin, return on assets, return on equity and cash flow margin. Secondary data was obtained from the following websites to report on Joint Commission Accreditation status, Hospital Consumer Assessment of Healthcare Providers and Systems star rating score and hospital financial performance for the nonprofit hospitals that participated in the study but did not report their performance measures.

The chapter was organized in a logical sequence to address the study's research questions and testing of the six hypotheses. The unpredictable nature of nonprofit hospitals was evaluated through the measured independent variables of hospital environmental turbulence, strategy aggressiveness, capability responsiveness, and strategic posture. In addition, nonprofit hospital's legitimacy was measured by evaluating the impact of their community programs, influence of governmental agencies, and culture on the nonprofit hospitals' performance.

A reactive to proactive Likert scale ranging from 1 to 5 was used to measure the independent strategic success model variables of environmental turbulence, strategic aggressiveness and capability responsiveness, legitimacy. The two gap variables, aggressiveness and responsiveness were calculated based on the responses to the survey questions relating to the gap variables. These variables represented the difference between strategic aggressiveness or capability responsiveness and environmental turbulence. A reactive to proactive Likert scale ranging from 1 to 5 was used to measure and evaluate the independent variables in the study. Nonprofit hospital's legitimacy was calculated by taking the average scores of the nonprofit hospital's community programs, influence of governmental agencies, and organizational culture and dividing them by the total number of legitimacy questions in order to evaluate the nonprofit hospital's legitimacy. The nonprofit hospital's strategic posture was evaluated by calculating the average scores of the nonprofit hospital's environmental turbulence, strategic aggressiveness, and capability responsiveness and dividing them by the total number of strategic aggressiveness, capability responsiveness and environmental turbulence questions.

Table 9 presents the descriptive statistics of the study's independent variables. The relationships among these variables were evaluated in SPSS, utilizing Spearman rho statistical analysis to compare the variables. All study results were tested at a 5% significance level for a 2-tailed distribution.

Descriptive Statistics of the Research Variables

Variable	Scale	Mean	St. Dev	Range	N
Nonprofit Hospital Environmental Turbulence	1 – 5	3.33	0.07	3.00	43
Nonprofit Hospital Strategy Aggressiveness	1 – 5	3.04	1.04	4.00	43
Nonprofit Hospital Capability Responsiveness	1 – 5	3.23	0.91	4.00	43
Nonprofit Hospital strategic posture	1 – 5	3.19	0.94	4.00	43
Nonprofit Hospital aggressiveness Gap	1 – 5	3.14	0.94	4.00	43
Nonprofit Hospital Responsiveness Gap	1 – 5	3.27	0.84	4.00	43
Nonprofit Hospital Legitimacy	1 – 5	3.04	0.91	4.00	43

Table 9

The nonprofit hospital's performance measures included the Joint Commission Accreditation, Hospital Consumer Assessment of Healthcare Providers and Systems (HCAHPS) scores, and financial performance was evaluated by averaging them over the five-year reporting period from 2013 to 2017. The nonprofit hospital's performance measures were evaluated using numerical data provided by one of the nonprofit hospital executives or staff with access to the hospital's performance data. Secondary data was utilized to report on the performance measures of the nonprofit hospitals that agreed to participate in the study.

The secondary data was gathered and reported from the Joint Commission Accreditation website at www.qualitycheck. org & Hospital Consumer Assessment of Healthcare Providers and Systems (HCAHPS) website at www.medicare.gov/ hospitalcompare and for the nonprofit hospital's financial performance from the American Hospital Directory website at www.ahd.com. Table 10 presents the descriptive statistics of the study's dependent (performance) variable independent variables. The relationships among these variables were evaluated in SPSS, utilizing Spearman rho and linear regression statistical analysis to compare the variables. All study results were tested at a 5% significance level for a 2-tailed distribution.

Descriptive Statistics for Performance Measures

Dependent Variable	Scale	Mean	St. Dev.	Range	N
Joint Commission Accreditation Score	1 – 5	4.33	1.29	4.00	43
Hospital Consumer Assessment of Healthcare Providers and Systems (HCAHPS)score	1 – 5	3.00	1.02	4.00	43
Average Operating Margin	Percent	0.11	0.56	3.56	43
Total Margin	Percent	0.02	0.03	0.14	43
Average Return on Assets (ROA)	Percent	0.05	0.08	0.48	43
Average Cash Flow Margin	Percent	0.23	0.84	4.71	43

Table 10

RESEARCH VARIABLE RESULTS

Hypothesis 1 (Not Supported)

Hypothesis 1 predicted a reliable relationship between the nonprofit hospital strategy aggressiveness gap and financial performance. Hypothesis 1 was analyzed using Spearman rho and did not show a statistical significance and was not supported $[r]=.239$ and $p = .122$, indicating there was not a reliable relationship between the nonprofit hospitals' strategic aggressiveness gap and their financial performance. A Spearman rho coefficient was calculated to determine whether a significant relationship existed between the nonprofit hospitals' strategic aggressiveness gap and financial performance. The relationship between the nonprofit hospitals' strategic aggressiveness gap and financial performance was examined and the statistical results did not show a significant relationship existed between the nonprofit hospital's strategic aggressiveness gap and financial performance. The statistical data shown in Table 11 demonstrate that as the nonprofit hospitals' strategic aggressiveness did not match their environmental turbulence and financial performance.

Hypothesis 2 (Supported)

Hypothesis 2 predicted a reliable relationship between the Nonprofit hospitals' capability responsiveness gap and their performance measure – Joint Commission Accreditation score and Hospital Consumer Assessment of Healthcare Providers & Systems (HCAHPS). Hypothesis 2 was supported ([r]=.322, p = .038; [r] = .352, p = .022), indicating there was a reliable relationship between the Nonprofit hospitals' capability responsiveness gap and quality performance measures - Joint Commission Accreditation and HCAHPS.

A Spearman rho coefficient was calculated to determine whether a significant relationship existed between the nonprofit hospitals' capability responsiveness gap and performance measures - Joint Commission Accreditation scores and HCAHPS scores. The statistical data shown in Table 11 shows the significance in the nonprofit hospital's capability responsiveness gap and the performance measures - Joint Commission on Accreditation and HCAHPS.

Hypothesis 3 (Supported)

Hypothesis 3 predicted a reliable relationship between the Nonprofit hospital capability responsiveness and performance measure Joint Commission Accreditation and Hospital Consumer Assessment of Healthcare Providers & Systems (HCAHPS). Hypothesis 3 was supported ([r]=.322, p = .038; [r] = .395, p = .022) indicating there was a significant relationship and correlation between the nonprofit hospitals' capability responsiveness and quality performance measures – Joint Commission Accreditation and Hospital Consumer Assessment of Healthcare Providers & Systems (HCAHPS). A Spearman rho correlation was calculated to determine whether a significant relationship existed between the nonprofit hospitals' capability responsiveness and quality performance measures of Joint Commission Accreditation and HCAHPS scores. The statistical data shown in Table 11 demonstrates the significance between the nonprofit hospitals' capability responsiveness quality performance measures - Joint Commission Accreditation and HCAHPS.

Hypothesis 4 (Not Supported)

Hypothesis 4 predicted a reliable relationship between the nonprofit hospitals' strategic aggressiveness and financial performance measure. Hypothesis 4 was not supported ($[r]$= .239, p = .122), indicating there was not a correlation or a reliable relationship between the nonprofit hospitals' strategic aggressiveness and financial performance.

A Spearman rho correlation was calculated to determine whether a correlation existed between the nonprofit hospitals' strategic aggressiveness and financial performance. Hypothesis 4 did not show a correlation between strategic aggressiveness and financial performance.

Hypothesis 5 (Supported)

Hypothesis 5 predicted that a reliable relationship existed between the nonprofit strategic posture and quality performance measure Joint Commission Accreditation. Hypothesis 5 was supported ($[r]$ = .321, p = .038), indicating there was a reliable relationship between the hospitals' strategic posture and quality performance measure Joint Commission Accreditation. A Spearman rho correlation was calculated and showed that a significant relationship did exist between nonprofit hospitals' strategic posture and the quality performance measure of Joint Commission Accreditation. Nonprofit hospitals that scored high on strategic posture also scored high on the Joint Commission Accreditation score.

Hypothesis 6 (Supported)

Hypothesis 6 predicted a reliable relationship existed between legitimacy and the quality performance measures of Joint Commission Accreditation and Hospital Consumer Assessment of Healthcare Providers & Systems (HCAHPS). Hypothesis 6 was supported ($[r] = .360$, $p = .018$; $[r] = .375$, $p = .013$), indicating there was a significant relationship between the nonprofit hospitals' legitimacy and the performance measures Joint Commission Accreditation & HCAHPS.

A Spearman rho correlation was calculated to determine whether a significant relationship existed between nonprofit hospitals' legitimacy and the performance measures of Joint Commission Accreditation Scores and Hospital Consumer Assessment of Healthcare Providers & Systems (HCAHPS). The nonprofit hospitals that scored high on legitimacy also scored high on the performance measures Joint Commission Accreditation & HCAHPS.

Hypothesis 7 (Supported)

Hypothesis 7 predicted a reliable relationship existed between environmental turbulence and strategic posture. Hypothesis 7 was supported ([r] = -.459, p = .002), indicating there was a significant relationship between the nonprofit hospitals' environmental turbulence and strategic posture. A Spearman rho correlation was calculated to determine whether a significant relationship existed between nonprofit hospitals' environmental turbulence and their strategic posture. The nonprofit hospitals' environmental turbulence did show significance with strategic posture.

SUMMARY OF RESULTS

The statistical analyses of the hypotheses and additional findings for this research were conducted using Spearman rho (r) and linear regression test. Spearman rho (r) is a non-parametric test used to measure the strength and direction associated between two ranked variables (Laerd Statistics, 2011). A linear regression analysis is a set of statistical processes for estimating the relationship among variables. It includes techniques for modeling and analyzing several variables, when the focus is on the relationship between a dependent variable and one or more independent variables (Laerd Statistics, 2011). All results were tested at a significance of 0.05. For Hypothesis 1, Nonprofit hospitals' strategic aggressiveness gap and financial performance was not supported. In Hypothesis

2, capability responsiveness gap and quality performance measures – Joint Commission Accreditation and Hospital Consumer Assessment of Healthcare Providers and Systems was supported. Hypotheses 3 relating to nonprofit hospitals' capability responsiveness and quality performance measures Joint Commission Accreditation and Hospital Consumer Assessment of Healthcare providers & Systems (HCAHPS) was supported. While Hypothesis 4 relating to strategic aggressiveness and financial performance was not supported. Hypothesis 5, strategic posture and quality performance measure – Joint Commission Accreditation was supported and Hypothesis 6 legitimacy and quality performance measures – Joint Commission Accreditation and Hospital Consumer Assessment of Healthcare Providers & Systems (HCAHPS) was supported. Hypothesis 7, environmental turbulence and strategic Posture was supported.

The statistical outcomes of this study are presented in Table 11.

Summary of Statistical Results

Hypotheses	Statistical Test	(rho) Value	P Value	Supported
H1. There is a reliable relationship between the nonprofit hospitals' strategic aggressiveness gap and financial performance measure	Spearman's rho	.239	.122	Not Supported
H2. There is a relationship between the nonprofit hospitals' capability responsiveness gap and quality performance measures (JCAHO & HCAHPS)	Spearman's rho (JCAHO)	.322	.038	Supported
	Spearman's rho (HCAHPS)	.352	.022	Supported
H3. There is a reliable relationship between nonprofit hospitals' capability responsiveness and quality performance measures (JCAHO & HCAHPS).	Spearman's rho (JCAHO)	.322	.038	Supported
	Spearman's rho (HCAHPS)	.352	.022	Supported
H4. There is a reliable relationship between the nonprofit hospitals' strategic aggressiveness and financial performance	Spearman's rho	.239	.122	Not supported
Q5. There is a relationship between nonprofit hospitals' strategic posture and performance measure of the Joint Commission Accreditation.	Spearman's rho	.321	.038	Supported
Q6. There is a reliable relationship between the nonprofit hospitals' legitimacy and performance measure of the Joint Commission Accreditation and HCAHPS.	Spearman's rho	.360	.018	Supported
		.375	.013	Supported
Q7. There is a reliable relationship between the nonprofit hospitals' environmental turbulence and strategic posture	Spearman's rho	-.459	.002	Supported

Table 11

ADDITIONAL RESEARCH FINDINGS

Correlations Among Other Research Variables

Table 12 presents the correlations among the other research variables that do not have hypotheses. There was significant correlation between the hospital's environmental turbulence and capability responsiveness ($r = .510$, $P = .001$); turbulence and strategic aggressiveness. Also, there was significant correlation between the performance measures Joint Commission Accreditation and Hospital Consumer Assessment of Healthcare Providers & Systems (HCAHPS) ($r = .378$, $p = .012$).

Both capability responsiveness and strategic aggressiveness does not have a significant relationship with financial performance of nonprofit hospitals. This was unexpectant since the introduction of new healthcare services, implementing new healthcare technology and strategy does impact the nonprofit hospital's financial performance. The reason there were no correlation between strategic aggressiveness gap and financial performance was because some of the financial data was negative and was numerical data whereas the strategic aggressiveness gap and strategy aggressiveness was ordinal data. This is the reason that there were no correlation between the variables in Hypotheses 1 and 4. If the financial data was ordinal and positive data the hypotheses would have been supported. Also, because the respondents were nonprofit federal, state or local government hospitals with medium turbulence levels that may have played a role in the nonprofit hospitals' financial performance not being correlated with the nonprofit hospitals' strategic aggressiveness and capability responsiveness gaps.

CORRELATIONS AMONG OTHER RESEARCH VARIABLES

		Strategic Aggressiveness	Capability Responsiveness
Environmental Turbulence	r	.422	.510
	P	.001	.001

Table 12

INTERCORRELATIONS BETWEEN STUDY VARIABLES

Table 13 reports the intercorrelations between the other study variables. As reported previously, p is significant at 0.05 or less, Hospital Consumer Assessment of Healthcare Providers & Systems (HCAHPS) scores was significantly correlated with the Joint Commission Accreditation performance measure.

In summary, both strategic aggressiveness and capability responsiveness gaps were not significantly correlated with the nonprofit hospital's financial performance, but both strategic aggressiveness and capability responsiveness were significantly correlated the Joint Commission Accreditation and Hospital Consumer Assessment of Healthcare Providers & Systems (HCAHPS) performance measures. Also, both strategic posture and legitimacy was significantly correlated with the nonprofit hospitals' Joint Commission Accreditation and HCAHPS performance measures. These were two important findings that emerged as related to the quality performance measures of the Joint Commission Accreditation and Hospital Consumer Assessment of Healthcare Providers & Systems (HCAHPS) scores over the five-year period from 2013 to 2017.

Overall the Joint Commission Accreditation and HCAHPS scores were significantly correlated and showed a strong relationship with most of the independent variables in the study.

Another important finding emerged as related to financial performance of nonprofit hospitals over the past five-year study period between 2013 to 2017 was that most of the nonprofit hospitals financial performance decreased from 2013 to 2017 and did not have a significant relationship with the independent variables of strategic aggressiveness or capability responsiveness. The only statistical correlation with financial performance was with the nonprofit hospitals return on assets and return on equity, but the operational margin, total margin, and cash flow margin was not correlated with any of the other financial performance measures. Also, the nonprofit hospitals' financial performance measure was negatively correlated with many of the independent variables.

Inter-correlations among the other research variables and performance measures

		Hospital Consumer Assessment of Healthcare Providers and Systems
Joint Commission Accreditation	r	-.507
	P	.001

Table 13

SUMMARY OF RESULTS

The statistical analyses of the hypotheses and additional findings for this research were conducted utilizing Spearman's rho (r) correlation and linear regression. Spearman's rho (r) is a nonparametric measure of correlation. It assesses how well a monotonic function could describe the relationship between two variables, without the assumption of frequency distribution of the variables.

All results were tested at a significance of < or = to 0.05. In Hypotheses 1, the nonprofit hospitals' strategic aggressiveness gap and performance measures: Joint Commission Accreditation, Hospital Consumer Assessment of Healthcare Provider & Systems, and financial performance was not supported. In Hypotheses 2, the nonprofit hospitals' capability responsiveness gap and performance measures: Joint Commission Accreditation and Hospital Consumer

Assessment of Healthcare Providers & Systems (HCAHPS) was supported and demonstrated a strong statistical significance and correlation. In Hypotheses 3, the nonprofit hospitals' capability responsiveness and the quality performance measures – Joint Commission Accreditation and Hospital Consumer Assessment of Healthcare Providers & Systems was supported and showed a statistical significance and correlation. In Hypothesis 4, the nonprofit hospitals' strategic aggressiveness and financial performance was not supported and did not show a statistical significance, but Hypothesis 5 and 6 was supported and did show a statistical significance. In Hypothesis 5, there was a reliable relationship between the nonprofit hospitals' strategic posture and the performance measure – Joint Commission Accreditation.

Hypothesis 6 showed a significant correlation between the nonprofit hospitals' legitimacy and performance measures – Joint Commission Accreditation and Hospital Consumer Assessment of Healthcare Providers & Systems (HCAHPS) scores. Hypothesis 7 showed a significant correlation between the nonprofit hospitals' environmental turbulence and strategic posture.

CHAPTER 5

SUMMARY, CONCLUSIONS AND RECOMMENDATIONS

*C*hapter 5 summarizes this research study's investigation of nonprofit hospitals strategic success factors (environmental turbulence, strategic aggressiveness and capability responsiveness) and the relationship between their performance measures (Joint Commission status, HCAHPS, and financial performance). Also, the study examined the relationship between nonprofit hospital's strategic posture & legitimacy and the impact on nonprofit hospitals' quality performance measures of Joint Commission Accreditation and Hospital Consumer Assessment of Healthcare Providers & Systems scores. This chapter briefly summarizes the background of the problem, purpose of the study, global and research models developed to investigate the strategic success factors and performance measures of nonprofit hospitals. It reviews the research variable, research findings, additional findings and conclusions. In addition, it elaborates on the contributions to the academic field of strategic management, contributions to the practice of strategic management for nonprofit hospitals and recommendations for further research.

BACKGROUND OF THE PROBLEM

During the past 20 to 30 years, the healthcare industry has changed dramatically and has taken on a whole new role in society. There have been countless improvements in modern medicine, and with the rapid changes in technology, public policy, and patient needs, healthcare and hospital costs has continued to skyrocket. We can compare healthcare costs today to those of 20 years ago as one way of illuminating the evolutionary changes in the United States healthcare system. We can go back to the end of 1999, when healthcare costs were over $1.07 trillion and accounted for only 14% of the U.S. Gross Domestic Product (GDP).

By the end of 2008, expenditures on healthcare in the United States had surpassed $2.3 trillion—more than twice the cost in 1999—and accounted for 16.2% of the nation's GDP. In 2016, healthcare costs rose to more than $3.6 trillion and accounted for over 18% of the nation's GDP (Munro, 2016). In 2021 it was $4.3 Trillion (www.ama-assn.org). This is the highest healthcare cost in all industrialized countries. Although the federal government and former President Obama passed a healthcare reform bill in 2010 healthcare costs has continued to rise. One of the major contributing factors to rising healthcare costs are hospital costs, which accounts for about 34% of all healthcare costs in the United States. Although hospitals have made improvements in reducing hospital cost for patients and insurances by reducing hospital in-patient length of stay and improving quality of care, hospitals costs continues to be one of the highest percentages of healthcare cost in the healthcare industry. Other contributing factors to rising hospital costs are an aging population, development of newer healthcare technology and an increase in patient and insurance companies demand for quality of care.

Due to the recent changes to the Affordable Care Act, healthcare policies and laws enacted by Congress has continued to increase hospital costs.

Nonprofit Hospital's performance measures have changed over the years, where quality of care, financial performance and patient satisfaction were not addressed or a concern for hospital management and executives. Over the past 15 to 20 years, this has changed and most nonprofit hospitals across the United States recognize they operate in an expeditiously changing environment. Hospital administrators understand that for their nonprofit hospitals to remain open their management teams must adapt to the changing environment and act more like a for-profit hospital. This research investigated the strategic behavior of nonprofit hospitals and their performance measures of quality (JCAHO and HCAHPS) and financial performance. In addition, it reviewed the strategic posture and legitimacy of the nonprofit hospitals and the effect on their performance measures.

STATEMENT OF THE PROBLEM

Hospital costs have continued to be the highest percentage of healthcare costs, accounting for more than 32% of all healthcare costs, or over $800 billion in 2012 (Martin, Lassman, Washington, & Catlin, 2013). By 2017, Hospital costs had exceeded $1 trillion and more than 34% of all health care costs in the United States. The previous economic recession, changing healthcare policies, increased public scrutiny of healthcare services and demand for quality has caused hospitals and other healthcare organizations to attempt to become more efficient.

Today, hospitals are investing in newer technology, adjusting provider compensation, changing strategies, increasing preventive care, and increasing community and patient involvement.

There is a need for more empirical research related to effective strategic success factors and performance in the healthcare industry. Also, there is a need to establish standardized quality and performance measurements for determining the success of nonprofit hospitals. Healthcare organizations will continue to need more effective strategic planning methods well into the future as hospital costs are projected to rise to 5.7% over the next decade and the demand for better quality of care continues to impact hospital performance. Historically, nonprofit hospitals have used a variety of different performance measures to determine success such as the Joint Commission on Accreditation of Hospitals, Lean Six Sigma criteria, Healthcare Effectiveness Data and Information Set (HEDIS), balanced scorecard, and other financial performance. Many of the performance measures in the hospital industry do not provide a concrete foundation or roadmap for the strategic success of nonprofit hospitals. Little is known about the impact of environmental factors on nonprofit hospitals, or how they respond to changes in the environment and other internal & external factors. The healthcare industry has undergone tremendous change over the past few decades, and nonprofit hospitals have been severely impacted with many of the smaller community hospitals being closed or having to merge with larger nonprofit hospitals.

PURPOSE OF THE STUDY

The study examined the relationship among the components of Dr. Ansoff's Strategic Success paradigm, strategic posture, legitimacy and performance measures in nonprofit hospitals.

The study hypothesized that the performance measures of nonprofit hospitals would improve when strategic aggressiveness, capability responsiveness are aligned with the hospital's environmental turbulence.

Also, the study hypothesized that nonprofit hospitals' strategic posture would correlate with the hospitals' quality performance measure, Joint Commission Accreditation and the nonprofit hospitals' performance measures of Joint Commission Accreditation and Hospital Consumer Assessment of Healthcare Providers & Systems would improve as the nonprofit hospitals' legitimacy improved.

EXPECTED CONTRIBUTIONS

The contribution of this study to the field of strategic management was to develop a framework representing an emerging theoretical perspective showing a relationship between Dr. Ansoff's Strategic Success Paradigm and the performance measures of nonprofit hospitals. The study provided researchers and hospital administrators with some tools for nonprofit hospitals can use to align their environment with their strategic thinking and capabilities to maximize their quality of care, patient satisfaction and financial sustainability.

Another contribution of this study was to provide a framework for nonprofit hospital administrators on ways their community involvement affects patient satisfaction and quality of care.

GLOBAL MODEL

The global model depicted in Figure 1 presented the comprehensive organizational factors affecting nonprofit hospitals. Figure 1 showed the strategic and operating behavior of hospitals/healthcare organizations. The left side of the global model shows the internal environmental factors and effecting nonprofit hospitals/healthcare organizations performance. The right side depicts the external environment and its relationship to hospital/healthcare organizations performance. Also, the global model illustrated Dr. Ansoff's strategic success factors and their relationship to the nonprofit hospitals/healthcare organizations.

Both left and right sides of the global model represented the global forces impacting hospitals' performance measures. It is a theoretical framework for evaluating the effectiveness of strategic management in healthcare and the challenges facing nonprofit hospitals/healthcare organizations. The strategic posture of the nonprofit hospitals was based on Dr. Ansoff's strategic success paradigm. The nonprofit hospital's strategic posture shown in the global model represents the nonprofit hospital's environmental turbulence, strategic aggressiveness, capability responsiveness, strategic intent and the interaction with the other external factors affecting nonprofit hospitals. Legitimacy shown in the global model illustrates the impact of government, legislation, and regulations on nonprofit hospital's legitimacy in their environment. Figure 1 below shows the global model with the internal and external factors affecting nonprofit hospitals.

GLOBAL MODEL

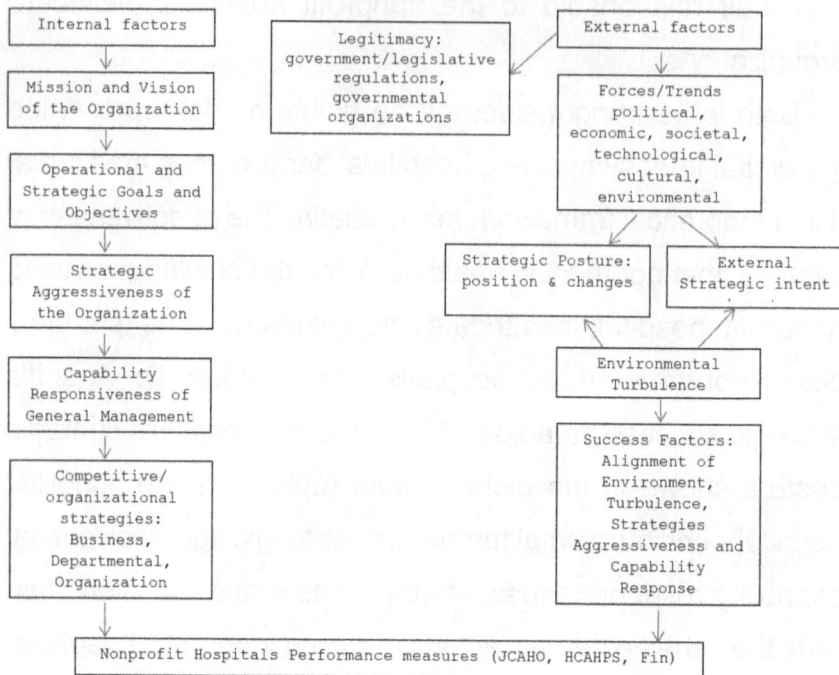

Figure 1. Global model

RESEARCH MODEL SUMMARY

The research model included Ansoff's Strategic Success Paradigm, strategic posture, legitimacy and their relationships with nonprofit hospital's performance measures of Joint Commission Accreditation, Hospital Consumer Assessment of Healthcare Providers & Systems (HCAHPS), and financial performance. Figure 2 represents the research model with segments of the internal and external factors affecting nonprofit hospitals. The research model shows the interaction between the nonprofit hospitals' strategic aggressiveness, capability responsiveness and environmental turbulence. Also, it illustrates the interaction between the nonprofit hospitals' strategic posture, legitimacy and the performance measures of the Joint Commission Accreditation and Hospital Consumer Assessment of Healthcare Providers & Systems.

RESEARCH MODEL

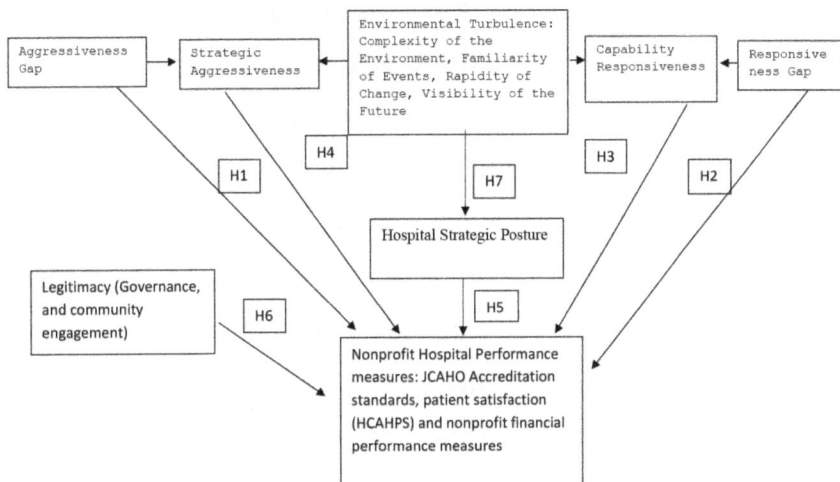

Figure 2. Research model.

SUMMARY OF RESEARCH VARIABLES

SUMMARY OF HOSPITAL ENVIRONMENTAL TURBULENCE

Ansoff (1979) defined environmental turbulence as the changeability, which includes complexity of the environment and novelty of change and predictability that includes rapidity of change and visibility of the future environment in which an organization operates. Turbulence for nonprofit hospitals is related to social needs, governmental regulations, organizational culture, economic and social change, competitive change, and complexity of the population the organization is serving. Social problems have been considered especially complex and turbulent as nonprofit hospitals are being hit hard with new federal and state regulations & policies. In addition, hospitals are seeing cuts and changes to federal, state and local funding and reimbursement rates from Medicare & Medicaid.

Some federal, state and local nonprofit hospitals have a greater turnover of employees, which would contribute to greater instability and thus increase turbulence levels for nonprofit hospitals. The stability and heterogeneity factors used in the definition of turbulence by Galaskiewicz and Shatin (1981) were integrated with Ansoff's (1979) environmental turbulence complexity definition for the current study. Novelty of change refers to changes in services, competition, legislation and technology. Rapidity of change references the speed of changes in services, legislation, technology or competition within the hospital industry.

SUMMARY OF HOSPITAL STRATEGIC AGGRESSIVENESS

Ansoff described strategic aggressiveness as the degree of discontinuity of the firm's successive strategic moves; and the timeliness of introduction of the organization's new products (1990).

Strategic aggressiveness for nonprofit hospitals is the intention of management to plan, innovate, and develop technology and services to meet patient needs in the local community and beyond.

The aggressiveness of nonprofit hospitals can range from stable to creative and the scale of discontinuity ranges from no change to creative change, which has not been observed previously. Increased costs of care are attributed to a variety of factors, but most commonly include the costs associated with new technology, innovative therapies, increased demand, and labor required to provide patient care (Bakera, Phibbs, Guarino, Supina, & Reynolds, 2004). Timeliness ranges from reactive to creative and trying innovative ways to meet patient needs.

SUMMARY OF HOSPITAL CAPABILITY RESPONSIVENESS

Capability responsiveness is characterized as the firm's ability to respond to changes in the environment and it includes the manager's capabilities and those of the organization. Ansoff and McDonnell (1990) characterized organizational responsiveness according to the manner in which a firm handles change. Nonprofit hospitals' capability responsiveness is the way management handles risk and change within the hospital's environment.

Responsiveness is characterized as the firm's responsiveness as the degree to which its organization is either introverted or extraverted and is identified by three components for the organization's capability responsiveness: Managers: Mentality, power, competency and capacity; climate: culture, risk propensity, time perspective, and change triggers; competence: problem-solving skills, information technology, organizational culture, and rewards.

This was consistent with the corresponding levels of turbulence and organizational responsiveness that Ansoff (1979) hypothesized for the Strategic Success Paradigm. When organizations were more strategic and open to risk and change, the organizations anticipated change sought to create new environments.

Some hospitals organized themselves with fewer goals, formalized roles and rules, and created boundaries despite the complexity. They sought stability and were more risk adverse. Yet the strong performers that responded to complex turbulence with strategic and structural complexity outperformed the other hospitals that responded with fewer goals and risk averseness. Ashmos et al. (2000) found the organizations that were more informal and had decentralized structures accepted risk and changeability more easily.

SUMMARY OF HOSPITAL LEGITIMACY

Many researchers have provided definitions of organizational legitimacy. Weber (1968) defined legitimacy as the valid domination that is then institutionalized with patterns of offices, rules, or procedures that validate the conformity and devotion of an organization's members.

Bell (1977) argued that legitimacy refers to an institution's extent of authority. Berger (1981) defined legitimacy as the rightful control of power; executives must assure the public that they use their power responsibly. They must command loyalty from the members of the organization and support from nonmembers. Ansoff and McDonnell (1990) defined legitimacy in terms of business as the degree of response of a firm's behavior to its stakeholders' expectations. They described legitimacy strategy as aspiration analysis, the impact of constraints, and the power field analysis of the organization (1990; p. 208).

Scott (1995) defined legitimacy as a condition reflecting cultural alignment, normative support, or consonance with relevant rules or laws (Scott, 1995; p. 45), depending on whether the emphasis is on cognitive, normative, or regulatory aspects of the healthcare organization. There are many sources of regulatory authority over hospitals, including common law, labor laws, personnel licensure, monitoring of financial operations, hospital licensure, and Medicaid/Medicare certification. White (2003) adopted a broad definition of legitimacy based on such authors as DiMaggio and Powell (1983), Scott (1992), Suchman (1995), and Zucker (1987) by including organizational culture, in addition to symbols, as a method to gain organizational support. He stated, "Legitimacy refers to the way organizational culture exists" (White, 2003; pp. 87-88). This cross-case analysis provides a unique view of legitimacy by explaining the intra-organizational relationship between the leaders of the hospital and culture. Hospitals are attempting to create a culture that defines itself with the inclusion of all organizational members, or to legitimize their organizations and their role. In terms of healthcare management, the hospital leaders first attempt to legitimize the ability of the hospital to improve the health of community members with its own improvement efforts. Secondly, hospital leaders legitimize their hospital's role as an influential and key decision maker and goal setter for care management in the organization. And lastly, all hospital leaders legitimize the existence of the hospital as an integrated organization focused on health and wellness of the community. Quality and performance measures should meet the needs of stakeholders and therefore should include clinical indicators of quality and indicators deemed important by the consumer (i.e. patient survey results, customer satisfaction). Although the evidence suggests that not-for-profit hospitals have become more businesslike and efficient, they have differentiated themselves by maintaining a higher level of community orientation.

Hospitals are concerned with their social legitimacy and the higher barriers for licensing, accreditation, and certificates. Hospitals can all attest to the institutional pressure from society due to the importance of the reputation of the services hospitals provide because most nonprofit hospitals are community hospitals, we assume legitimacy to be primarily a local issue instead of a regional or global issue. Hospitals improve their survival chances insofar, as they are successful in obtaining legitimacy from such normative sources such as the Joint Commission on Accreditation of Healthcare Organizations (JCAHO), the Centers for Medicare and Medicaid Services through the Hospital Consumer Assessment of Healthcare Providers & Systems (HCAHPS). The American Hospital Association (AHA) have argued that organizations operating in highly institutionalized environments are more likely to survive to the extent that they are successful in obtaining legitimacy from those normative sources that are able to approve or disapprove their structures, staffing, and programs. Institutional theory defines legitimacy as it relates to the community benefits that hospitals provide. Based on research of the different types of legitimacy, my research focused on various aspects of legitimacy in nonprofit hospitals that included organizational culture, management culture, interdependence, community involvement and patient satisfaction.

SUMMARY OF HOSPITAL STRATEGIC POSTURE

While strategic posture is defined as the approach leaders take in applying their strengths to the current and long-term needs of the marketplace. Formulating a strategic posture is part of the broader strategic planning process, when managers collaborate to develop the vision, goals, and strategies for the future (Kokemuller, 2014).

Dr. Ansoff defined strategic posture analysis as a descriptive and prescriptive tool used to measure the size of the gap between turbulence, strategy, and capability (Ansoff,

McDonnell, 1990). In these times of uncertainty, hospitals and health systems should be actively working on four major strategies to be positioned for the future. These groupings of strategies include: Growth, Effectiveness, Relevance and Capabilities. While growth and effectiveness strategies have been a staple of every health care organization strategic plans over the past two decades, the industry turbulence brings into increasing importance the strategies related to relevance and capabilities. To remain relevant, hospitals and health systems must reinvent themselves. This reinvention is particularly the case where consumer demands have shifted, technology has created viable substitutes and reimbursement changes the way value is monetized. In a changing world, hospitals will need to better articulate their relevance to their customers, patients, providers or payors. In the presence of a changing healthcare delivery system, hospitals will likely need to evaluate their community orientation and financing requirements for providing care. Results from a 2009 long-term study of the hospital industry showed that not-for-profit hospitals have been forced to emulate for-profit hospitals by becoming more business-like due to sweeping changes in the structure of the healthcare industry, multiple changes in healthcare policy, and pressure from patients and insurers, who are calling for the integration of healthcare quality with broader public and community health objectives.

Nonprofit hospitals with a high degree of community orientation may be well positioned to design and implement programs, target specific populations through knowledge of their community, identify gaps in care, and align with other healthcare organizations' strategies for improving overall healthcare quality in the community.

The business strategy is manifested in the alignment of a healthcare organization with its external environment. The organization aligns itself by establishing linkages with external parties to secure the resources that it needs to survive and by making internal structural adjustments. For the organization to be properly aligned, its organizational strategy should represent an internally consistent configuration of functional area strategies. Thus, one would expect that an organization's strategy in the functional area of finance should be consistent with its overall business strategy (Coddington, Fischer, Moore 2001).

SUMMARY OF HOSPITAL
PERFORMANCE MEASURES

The performance of nonprofit hospitals reflects a large variety of measurement tools to measure performance in these types of healthcare organizations, but one first must analyze the type of healthcare organizations being measured.

The types of nonprofit hospitals and health systems that was analyzed in this study was government, state, local community, and teaching hospitals and healthcare systems. The government, state, local community, and teaching nonprofit hospitals included small, medium, and large-sized acute care federal, state, local government and teaching hospitals and healthcare systems. For-profit, Mental health/Psychiatric, military and veteran administration (VA) hospitals were exempted from the study.

The nonprofit hospitals types were classified based on the following criteria.

- Nonprofit Community hospitals or health systems are classified as voluntary other or voluntary church-owned nonprofit hospitals.
- Government nonprofit community hospitals or health systems are classified as Federal or state governmental community hospitals and does not include Veteran Administration or Psychiatric or mental health hospital.

The performance measures chosen were based on research of the most common nonprofit hospital performance measures and from previous studies analyzing performance measures of nonprofit hospitals. The quality performance measure analyzed was the Joint Commission accreditation of Healthcare Organizations. The Joint Commission Accreditation standards measures quality, timeliness and effectiveness of healthcare delivered to patients by the hospital or health system. The Joint Commission Accreditation scores range from accredited or accredited with follow-up survey or preliminary denial of accreditation or denial of accreditation. Accredited is defined as the nonprofit hospital following all quality standards of healthcare or has successfully addressed requirements for improvement in an evidence of standards compliance within 45 or 60 days following the posting of the Accreditation Summary Findings Reports. Accreditation with follow-up survey is when the hospital is not in compliance with specific standards that require a follow-up survey be conducted within 30 days to 6 months.

Preliminary denial of accreditation is when there is justification to deny accreditation to a health care organization due to one or more of the following: an immediate threat to health or safety for patients or the public;

Submission of falsified documents or misrepresented information, lack of a required license or similar issue at the time of the survey, failure to resolve the requirements of an Accreditation with follow-up survey status; patients having been placed at risk for serious adverse outcomes due to significant or pervasive patterns/trends/repeat findings, or significant noncompliance with joint commission standards. Denial of accreditation results when a hospital has been denied accreditation and all review and appeal opportunities have been exhausted (JCAHO, 2018). Nonprofit hospitals have accreditation inspections every 3 years unless they are denied accreditation by the Joint Commission. The Hospital Consumer Assessment of Healthcare Providers and Systems (HCAHPS) rating scores is a national, standardized, publicly-reported survey of patients' perspectives of quality of hospital care. The HCAHPS scores are designed and intended for use at the hospital level for comparing hospitals to each other. HCAHPS survey asks recently discharged patients about aspects of their hospital experience that they are uniquely suited to address. HCAHPS is administered to a random sample of adult inpatients between 48 hours and six weeks after discharge from a hospital. HCAHPS Star-Rating provides consumers with a simple overall rating generated by combining multiple dimensions of quality into a single summary rating score. The HCAHPS summary star rating combines information about different aspects of patient experience of care. The HCAHPS summary star rating is constructed from the following components. The seven-star ratings from each of the 9 HCAHPS composite measures that include nurse communication, doctor communication, responsiveness of hospital staff, pain management, communication about medicines, discharge information, and care transition. The HCAHPS summary star rating is the average of the 9 composite measure star ratings, the star rating for HCAHPS individual items, and the star rating for HCAHPS global items. The nonprofit hospital financial performance measures (Operating margin, total margin, return on equity, return on assets and cash flow margin) helped determine the hospital's financial viability and efficiency. For nonprofit hospital, retained earnings, return on equity represent one of the most important sources of financial viability (Singh, Wheeler, 2012). Managing the flow of patients, through the hospital, revenue cycle effectiveness is directly linked with improved profitability and equity growth in nonprofit hospitals. Thus, higher net patient revenue and lower operating expenses result in higher operating and total margins, thus improving a hospital's sustainability and allowing it to build equity. Cash flow margin is based on the nonprofit hospital's net income minus other several other financial markers divided by net patient revenue plus other income minus other financial factors and plays an important role in estimating a hospital's equity value and financial viability.

The Joint Commission accreditation scores for nonprofit hospitals was used as one of the performance measurements to determine quality of care performance. Another was the Hospital Consumer Assessment of Healthcare Providers and Systems (HCAHPS) rating scores to determine coverall hospital quality of services and patient satisfaction.

Financial performance determined the nonprofit hospital's financial sustainability and viability. The criteria used for the Joint Commission was each nonprofit hospital's accreditation final performance scores that was obtained through the Joint Commission's website at www.qualitycheck.org or at the American Hospital Directory website at www.ahd.org. The other criteria was the nonprofit hospital's consumer assessment of healthcare providers and systems survey (HCAHPS), which measure patient satisfaction rating scores obtained through the hospital compare website at https://www.medicare.gov/hospitalcompare/search.html.

The criteria used to measure the nonprofit hospital's financial performance were the hospital's operating margin, total margin, return on equity (ROE), return on assets, and cash flow margin. Nonprofit hospital's return on assets is defined as net income divided by total assets and cash flow margin is net income + interest + depreciation divided by total revenue.

Among the five indicators were operating margin, total margin, cash flow ratio, return on equity and return on assets.

Operating margin. Operating margin (OM), measures the control of operating expenses relative to operating revenue (net patient and other revenue). A positive value indicates operating expenses are less than operating revenue, which is net patient revenue minus total operating expense, which gives the net operating income indicating profits solely from a hospital's operations (Nowicki, 2015).

Total margin is a measure of hospital financial performance that measures nonprofit hospital's net operating income divided by their total revenue.

Return on Equity (ROE) focus is on both short and long-term results. ROE is a function of margin multiplied by leverage multiplied by turnover. ROE for nonprofit hospitals is calculated as net income divided by total equity (total assets minus total liabilities).

Return on assets (ROA) is net income divided by total assets and

Cash Flow Margin is the hospital's net income minus (contributions, investments and appropriations) plus depreciation plus interest divided by net patient revenue plus other income minus (contributions, investments, and appropriations) or total revenue.

Cash flow margin is a ratio of the sum of net income and depreciation expense to total revenue (Zhao et al., 2008).

DISCUSSION OF FINDINGS

The nonprofit hospital's environmental turbulence, strategic aggressiveness, capability responsiveness, strategic posture, legitimacy and performance were computed from responses to the corresponding survey questions related to each variable. The strategic aggressiveness gap and capability responsiveness gap was calculated as the difference between the nonprofit hospitals' environmental turbulence and their strategic aggressiveness and capability responsiveness. The summary of the results of Hypothesis 1 did not show statistical significance and correlation between nonprofit hospitals' strategic aggressiveness gap and financial performance measure.

Hypothesis 2 did show a significant relation between the nonprofit hospitals' capability responsiveness gap and quality performance measures – Joint Commission Accreditation and Hospital Consumer Assessment of Healthcare Providers & Systems (HCAHPS). Hypothesis 3 did show a significant relationship between capability responsiveness and quality performance measures – Joint Commission Accreditation and Hospital Consumer Assessment of Healthcare Providers & Systems (HCAHPS).

Hypothesis 4 did not show significance and correlation between strategic aggressiveness and financial performance.

Hypotheses 5 and 6 showed statistical significance and correlation between the nonprofit hospitals' strategic posture and quality performance measure – Joint Commission Accreditation and legitimacy & quality performance measures of Joint Commission Accreditation and Hospital Consumer Assessment of Healthcare Providers & Systems (HCAHPS). In addition, the Hypothesis 7 did show significance and a reliable relationship between the nonprofit hospitals' environmental turbulence and strategic posture.

Based on the results of the survey, many nonprofit hospitals' environmental turbulence ranged from changing to surprising due to changes in policies, development of newer healthcare technology, new regulations and uncertainty surrounding the Affordable Care Act.

The sample sizes, means, standard deviations, and reliability outcome pertaining to the variables were presented in Table 11. Spearman's rho revealed statistical correlation for Hypotheses 1 thru 7 with a significance level less than .05.

The research findings also showed a significant relationship between strategic aggressiveness and capability responsiveness (r = .691, p = .003) and a significant relationship between capability responsiveness and legitimacy. The level of environmental turbulence of nonprofit hospitals varies depending on the size and location of the hospital. The unpredictable nature of hospitals was apparent as several nonprofit hospitals are being forced to merge or partner with other hospitals to remain open.

Summary of Statistical Results

Hypotheses	Statistical Test	(rho) Value	P Value	Supported
H1. There is a reliable relationship between the nonprofit hospitals' strategic aggressiveness gap and financial performance measure	Spearman's rho	.239	.122	Not Supported
H2. There is a relationship between the nonprofit hospitals' capability responsiveness gap and performance measures (JCAHO & HCAHPS)	Spearman's rho (JCAHO)	.322	.038	Supported
	Spearman's rho (HCAHPS)	.352	.022	Supported
H3. There is a reliable relationship between nonprofit hospitals' capability responsiveness and performance measures (JCAHO & HCAHPS).	Spearman's rho (JCAHO)	.322	.038	Supported
	Spearman's rho (HCAHPS)	.352	.022	Supported
H4. There is a reliable relationship between the nonprofit hospitals' strategic aggressiveness and financial performance	Spearman's rho	.239	.122	Not supported
Q5. There is a relationship between the nonprofit hospitals' strategic posture and performance measures of the Joint Commission Accreditation and HCAHPS.	Spearman's rho	.321	.038	Supported
Q6. There is a reliable relationship between the nonprofit hospitals' legitimacy and performance measures of Joint Commission Accreditation and HCAHPS	Spearman's rho	.360	.018	Supported
Q7. There is a reliable relationship between the nonprofit hospitals' environmental turbulence and strategic posture	Spearman's rho	-.459	.002	Supported

Table 14

ADDITIONAL FINDINGS

Table 14 presents the correlations among the other research variables that do not have hypotheses. There was significant correlation the hospital's environmental turbulence and capability responsiveness (r = .510, P = .001) turbulence and strategic aggressiveness. Also, there was significant correlation between the performance measure of Joint Commission Accreditation and Hospital Consumer Assessment of Healthcare Providers & Systems (HCAHPS) (r = .378, p = .012).

Both capability responsiveness and strategic aggressiveness does not have a significant relationship with financial performance of nonprofit hospitals. This was unexpectant since the introduction of new healthcare services, implementing new healthcare technology and strategy does impact the nonprofit hospital's financial performance. I believe because the financial data was not ordinal and put into a range from low to high financial performance (Likert scale) that many of the participants may have over or under estimated their financial data. Also, because the respondents were nonprofit federal, state or local government hospitals with medium turbulence levels that may have played a role in the nonprofit hospitals' financial performance not being significantly correlated with the nonprofit hospitals' strategic aggressiveness and capability responsiveness gaps.

CONCLUSIONS

The study examined the relationships between nonprofit hospitals environmental turbulence, strategy aggressiveness, capability responsiveness, strategic posture, and the quality and financial performance of nonprofit hospitals throughout the United States.

The study hypothesized that the nonprofit hospital's quality performance measures and financial performance would improve when strategy aggressiveness and capability responsiveness were aligned with the hospital's turbulence level. Based on the Spearman rho statistical test that showed significant correlation existed between quality performance measures of Joint Commission and Hospital Consumer Assessment of Healthcare Providers & Systems and capability responsiveness when the hospital's turbulence level were aligned. Also, the study hypothesized that quality performance measures of Joint Commission Accreditation and Hospital Consumer Assessment of Healthcare Providers & Systems would be significantly correlated with strategic posture measures. There was a positive relationship with quality performance measures and strategic posture. In addition, there was a strong positive correlation between the nonprofit hospital's legitimacy and quality performance measures. Based on the findings of this research study, nonprofit hospitals could improve their strategy and capabilities to improve their financial performance. In addition to these findings, nonprofit hospitals did show that strategy aggressiveness and quality performance measures showed a positive and significant relationship along with capability responsiveness. Other statistical findings showed a negative relationship between strategic aggressiveness and financial performance. Also, a negative relationship between strategy aggressiveness and financial performance.

RECOMMENDATIONS FOR HOSPITAL EXECUTIVES

The research study examined Dr. Ansoff's strategic success paradigm with nonprofit hospitals and their performance measures. Based on the results of the study, hospital executives could improve their strategy aggressiveness, improve their capability responsiveness to adapt to a rapidly changing environment.

Also, nonprofit hospitals need to act more like for-profit hospitals and develop strategies to address some of the gaps in their environment and with their community programs. In addition, healthcare executives need to be more engaged with their regulatory agencies, community involvement and performance measures for them to remain open or sustain their viability and financial security. It is imperative that healthcare management continuously analyze their environments, develop sound strategies for addressing the changes in the environment.

CONTRIBUTIONS TO THE ACADEMIC FIELD OF STRATEGIC MANAGEMENT

The study contributed to the academic field of strategic management by testing and validating Dr. Ansoff's strategic success paradigm in the nonprofit hospital industry. It empirically showed the relationship between environmental turbulence, capability responsiveness and the quality performance measures for nonprofit hospitals. Also, it showed the strong relationship between nonprofit hospital's legitimacy and the quality of care performance measure. The study provided researchers, healthcare executives with additional tools for aligning their environment with their strategic aggressiveness, capability responsiveness and legitimacy to improve the performance outcomes any environment.

This research further validated the application of Dr. Ansoff's strategic success paradigm by validating it's applicability in the nonprofit hospital industry and complemented the works of Dr. Greg Lorton's environmental systems integration (2006) and Dr. Victor Muglia's Relationship between environmental turbulence, management support, organizational collaboration, information technology solution realization, and process performance in healthcare provider organizations (2010).

CONTRIBUTIONS TO THE PRACTICE
OF STRATEGIC MANAGEMENT

The study contributed to the practice of strategic management by demonstrating the connection between Dr. Ansoff's strategic success factors and hospital strategic management. It showed that Dr. Ansoff's strategic success paradigm can be applied in the hospital industry to influence performance outcomes of nonprofit hospitals. The study summarized the strategic success paradigm as a framework for healthcare executives to integrate their strategies and capabilities within the nonprofit hospitals' environment to maximize their performance outcomes. Also, the study provided a foundation for nonprofit hospitals to improve their patient satisfaction scores (HCAHPS) and other performance measures to improve their quality and financial performance.

RECOMMENDATIONS FOR FURTHER RESEARCH

The research study could be refined and expanded for further research. The following are additional items to be considered for further research:

1. Additional respondents to the research study would have allowed for a larger sample size would have provided stronger correlations between the variables.
2. Additional questions could have been designed and added that pertained to environmental turbulence and strategy aggressiveness. The reliability for Cronbach's alpha coefficient = .56 is low and more questions could have increased the reliability coefficient to support consistency.
3. Omitting the financial performance questions and just leaving the Joint Commission and HCAHPS performance questions.

Further research is recommended to identify other internal and external factors impacting nonprofit hospitals performance. My research only studied some of the internal and external factors affecting performance outcomes of nonprofit hospitals.

REFERENCES

Aday, L. A., Begley, C. E., Lairson, D. R., & Slater, C. H. (1999). Evaluating the healthcare system: Effectiveness, efficiency, and equity. *Journal of Policy Analysis and Management, 18*, 713.

Al-Amin, M., Makarem, S. C. (2016). The Effects of Hospital-Level Factors Patients' Ratings of Physician Communication. *Journal of Healthcare Management*, Vol 61(1), pp. 28 – 43.

Aldrich, R. (1999). Hospital Mergers. *Journal of Healthcare Management*, Vol 44 (5), pp. 380.

American Hospital Association. (2014*). Hospital statistics.* Chicago, IL: American Hospital Association Press.

Anderson, R. M., Rice, T. H., Kominski, G. F. (2001). Changing the U.S. Healthcare system: *Key Issues in Health Services Policy and Management.* San Francisco, CA: Jossey-Bass Pub.

Angermeier, I., Dunford, B. B., Boss, A. D., Boss, R. W. (2009). The Impact of Participative Management Perceptions on Customer Service, Medical Errors, Burnout, and Turnover Intentions *Journal of Healthcare Management* 54(2)

Ansoff, I. H. (1987). The emerging paradigm of strategic behavior. *Strategic Management Journal, 8*, 501-515.

Ansoff, I. H.(1993). Optimizing profitability in turbulent environments: A formula for strategic success. *Long Range Planning, 26*, 11-23.

Ansoff, I. H., & McDonnell, E. J. (1990). *Implanting strategic management* (2nd ed.). NJ: Prentice Hall.

Ansoff, I. H., & Sullivan, P. A. (1991). Strategic responses to environmental turbulence. In R. H. Kilmann, I. Kilmann, & Associates (Eds.). *Making organizations competitive.* San Francisco, CA: Jossey-Bass.

Ansoff, I. H. & Sullivan, P. A.(1993). Empirical support for a paradigmic Theory of strategic success behaviors in environment-serving Organizations. *International Review of Strategic Management, 4*, 173-203.

Armit, K. (2015). Evidence, Culture and Clinical Outcome. *Future Hospital Journal,* Vol 2 (3), 194-196.

Author, J., (2011). *Lean Six Sigma for Hospital: Simple Steps to Fast Affordable, Flawless Healthcare.* Chicago, IL: McGraw Hill.

Barnet, S., (2015). Hospital Innovation Centers Think Outside the Box to Solve Healthcare's Biggest Problems. *Hospital Review*, 10, 10–12.

Bazzoli, G. J., (2004). The Corporatization of American Hospitals. *Journal of Health politics, policy & law*, 29(5), 885-905.

Beasley, S. A., (2010). A brief guide to the U.S. Health Care Delivery System. Chicago, IL: *American Hospital Association Press*.

Begun, J., and Heatwole, K. B., (1999). Strategic Cycling: Shaking Complacency in Healthcare Strategic Planning. *Journal of Healthcare Management* 44 (5): 339-51.

Bennett, A. R., (2012). Accountable Care Organizations: Principles and Implications for Hospital Administrators. *Journal of Healthcare Management*, Vol. 57 (4), pg.244-254

Bigelow, B., & Arndt, M.(2005). Transformational change in health care: Changing the question. *Hospital Topics, 83*(2), 19-26.

Blumenthal, D. (2017). How the New U.S. Tax Plan Will Affect Health Care. *Harvard Business Review*: Retrieved from https://hbr.org/2017/12/how-the-new-u-s-tax-plan-will-affect-health-care.

Bryson, J. M.(1995). *Strategic planning for public and nonprofit Organizations: A guide to strengthening and sustaining organizational achievement.* San Francisco, CA: Jossey-Bass.

Butler, G., Caldwell, C., (2008). *What Top-Performing Healthcare Organizations Know: 7 Proven Steps for Accelerating and Achieving Change.* Chicago, IL: Health Administration Press.

Butcher, L. (2015). Exceptional Experiences (without exception): Low Patient Scores Can Hurt Your Reputation and Your Bottom Line. *Hospitals & Health Networks*, pp. 38-42.

Byrd, J. D., Landry, A., (2012). Distinguishing Community Benefits: Tax Exemption Versus Organizational Legitimacy. *Journal of Healthcare Management*, 57(1), pg. 66 -76

Carman, K. (2006). *The relationship among environmental turbulence, Strategic behavior, competitive posture and performance: The case of State and federally chartered credit unions* (Unpublished doctoral dissertation). Alliant International University, San Diego, CA.

Clarke, S., and J. Oakley. 2007. Informed Consent and Clinician Accountability: The Ethics of Report Cards on Surgeon Performance. Cambridge, MA: *Cambridge University Press*. Epstein, A.

Coats, K. (2010). Practitioner Application. *Journal of Healthcare Management*, 55 (1).

Coddington, D. C., Fischer, E. A., & Moore, K. D.(2001). *Strategies for the new health care marketplace: Managing the convergence of consumerism and technology.* San Francisco, CA: Jossey-Bass.

Coile, R. C., Jr.(2002). Futurescan 2002: *A forecast of healthcare trends 2002 - 2006.* Chicago, IL: Health Administration Press.

Collum, T., Menachemi, N., Kilgore, M., Weech-Maldonado, R., (2014). Management Involvement on the Board of Directors and Hospital Financial Performance. *Journal of Healthcare Management*, VOL 59 (6), PP. 429-45

Creswell, J., Abelson, R. (2013). New Laws and Rising Costs Create a Surge Of Supersizing Hospitals, *New York Times*. Retrieved from http://www.nytimes.com/2013/08/13/business/bigger-hospitals-may-lead-to-bigger-bills-for-patients.html

Cutler, D. M. (2000*). The changing hospital industry: Comparing not- for-profit and for-profit institutions.* Chicago, IL: University of Chicago.

Daly, R. (2016). NFP Hospitals Improved Revenue, Profitability in 2015. *Hospital Financial Management Association*, White Paper

Dart, R. C. (2011). Can Lean Thinking Transform American Healthcare? *Annals of Emergency Medicine*, Vol 57, pp. 279-81

Devers, K. J., Brewster, L. R., Casalino, L. P. (2003). Changes in Hospital Competitive Strategy: A New Medical Arms Race. *Health Services Research*, 38 (1): 447-70.

De Souza, L. B. (2009). Trends and Approaches in Lean Healthcare. *Leadership in Health Services*, Vol 22, pp 121-39.

Diana, M. L., Harle, C. A., Huerta, T. R., Ford, E. W., & Menachemi, N. (2014). Hospital characteristics associated with achievement of meaningful use. *Journal of Healthcare Management, 59*(4).

Dlugacz, Y. D., Restifo, A., & Greenwood, A.(2004). *The quality handbook for health care organizations: A manager's guide to tools and programs.* San Francisco, CA: Jossey-Bass.

Dong, G. N. (2016). Earnings Management in U.S. Hospitals. *Journal of Health and Human Services Administration.* 39(1).

Drell, L., Davis, J. (2014). Getting Started with Predictive Analytics. *Marketing Health Services*, 34(3), pp. 22-5

Drucker, P. F.(1990). *Managing the non-profit organization: Principles and practices.* New York, NY: HarperCollins.

Eickhoff, K. F., Plowman, D. A., McDaniel, R. R., (2011). Hospital Boards and Hospital Strategic Focus: The impact of Board Involvement in Strategic Decision Making. *Healthcare Management Review*, 36(2)

Ellison, A., Cohen, J. K., (2017). 230 Hospital Benchmarks. *Becker's Hospital Review.* May 2017.

Fennell, M. L., Adams, C. M., (2011). U.S. Health-Care Organizations: Complexity, Turbulence, and Multilevel Change. *Annual Review of Sociology*, (37): 205-219.

Finlayson, E., J. Birkmeyer, D. Baker, et al. 2002 "Should Consumers Trust Hospital Quality Report Cards?" *JAMA* 287 (24): 3206-08.

Ford, R., Boss, R. W., Angermeier, I., Townson, C. D., Jennings, T. A. (2004). Adapting to Change in Healthcare: Aligning Strategic Intent And Operational Capacity. *Hospital Topics*, Vol 82 (4), pp. 20-9

Freed, D. H. (2005). *Hospital Turnarounds: Agents, Approaches, Alchemy. The Health Care Manager* 24 (2): 96 – 118

Friedman, L. H., Corvallis, Goes, J. B., (2000). The Timing of Medical Technology Acquisition: Strategic Making in turbulent Environments. *Journal of Healthcare Management*, 45(5)

Ginn, G. O., Shen, J. J., Moseley, C. B., (2009). Community Orientation And the Strategic Posture of Hospitals. *Hospital Topics*, 87(3)

Gish, R. (2002). Measuring Strategic Success. *Healthcare Financial Management Association*, 56(8), pp. 34-37.

Glassman, A.M., Zell, D., & Duron, S. (2005). Thinking Strategically in Turbulent times. Armonk, NY: M.E. Sharp

Goozner, M. (2014). Fostering a place where employees can excel. *Modern Healthcare, 44*(43).

Greene, J. (2009). The New Pace of Strategic Planning. *Hospitals & Health Networks, Health Forum*.

Griffith, J. R., White, K. R. (2011). *Reaching Excellence in Healthcare Management*. Chicago, IL: Health Administration Press

Grube, M. E. (2015). Making the case for virtual healthcare. *Healthcare Executive Magazine, 30*(2).

Hacker, K., Walker, D. K. (2013). Achieving Population Health in Accountable Care Organizations. *American Journal of Public Health*, 103(7), pp. 1163-1167.

Hartman, M., Martin, A. B., Lassman, D., Catlin, A., (2014). National health spending in 2013: Growth slows, remains in step with the overall economy. *Health Affairs Journal, 33*(12).

Hoffman, A., & Emanuel, E. J. (2013). Reengineering US health care. *Journal of the American Medical Association, 309*(7), 661-662.

Holmes, G. M., Pink G. H. (2012). Adoption and Perceived Effectiveness of Financial Improvement Strategies in Critical Access Hospitals. *Journal of Rural Health*, 28 (1), pp. 92-100.

Jegers, M. (2009). Corporate governance in nonprofit organizations. *Nonprofit Management & Leadership, 20*(2), 143-164.

Joint Commission on Accreditation of Healthcare Organizations. (2014). *2014 hospital accreditation standards*. Oakbrook, IL: Joint Commission Resources.

Joshi, M. S., Horak, B. J., (2010). Care Coordination. Trustee: *Journal of Hospital Governing Boards*, 63(6).

Kaissi, A. A., Begun, J. W., Hamilton, J. A., (2008). Strategic Planning Processes and Hospital Financial Performance. *Journal of Healthcare Management*, 53(3).

Kang, R., Hasnain-Wynia, R., (2013). Hospital Commitment to Community Orientation and Its Association with Quality of Care and Patient Experience. *Journal of Healthcare Management*, 58(4).

Kaplan, R. S., Witkowski, M., Abbott, M., Guzman, A. B., Higgins, L. D., Meara, J. G., Feeley, T. W., (2014). Using Time-Driven Activity-Based Costing to identify Value Improvement Opportunities in Healthcare. *Journal of Healthcare Management*, 59(6).

Kash, B. A., Spaulding, A., Johnson, C. E., Gamm, L., (2014). Editorial. *Journal of Healthcare Management*, 61(6), 383.

Kaufman, B. G., Thomas, S. R., Randolph, R. K., Perry, J. R., Thompson, K. W., Holmes, G. M., Pink, G. H. (2016). The Rising Rate Of Rural Hospital Closures. *Journal of Rural Health*, Vol. 32 (1), pp. 35-43.

Kelly, D. (2008). *Human service sector nonprofit organizations' social impact and the relationship to strategic success* (Unpublished doctoral dissertation). Alliant International University, San Diego, CA.

Kim, C. S., Spahlinger, D. A., Kin, J. M., Coffey, R. J., Billi, J. E. (2009). Implementation of Lean Thinking: One Health System's Journey. *Joint Commission Journal on Quality and Patient Safety* Vol 35: Pp 406-413.

Kim, T. H., Thompson, J. M. (2012). Organizational and Market Factors Associated with Leadership Development Programs in Hospitals: A National Study. *Journal of Healthcare Management*, 57(2)

Kirby, P. B., Spetz, J., Maiuro, L., Scheffler, R. M. (2006). Changes in Service Availability in California Hospitals, 1995 to 200. *Journal Of Healthcare Management*, 51(1).

Kirk, M. A., Holmes, G. M., Pink, G. H. (2012). Achieving Benchmark Financial Performance in CAHs: Lessons from High Performers. *Journal of the Healthcare Financial Management Association*, 66 (4), pp. 116-20

Kollberg, B., Dahlgaard, J. J., Brehmer, P. O. (2006). Measuring Lean Initiatives in Healthcare Services: Issues and Findings. *International Journal of Productivity and Performance Management*, 56:7-24.

Langabeer, J. (1998). Competitive Strategy in Turbulent Healthcare Markets: An Analysis of Financially Effective Teaching Hospitals. *Journal of Healthcare Management*, 43(6).

Leonardi, M.]., M. L. McGory, and C. Y. Ko. 2007. "Publicly Available Hospital Comparison Web Sites: Determination of Useful, Valid, and Appropriate Information for Comparing Surgical Quality." Archives of Surgery 142 (9): 863-68.

Longest, B. B. (2012). Management Challenges at the Intersection of Public Policy Environments and Strategic Decision Making in Public Hospitals *Journal of Health and Human Services Administration.*

Longest, B. B. (2010). *Health Policymaking in the United States,* (5th ed.). Chicago: Health Administration Press.

Lorton, G. A. (2006). *Factors relating environmental management strategies And performance on environmental issues* (Unpublished doctoral dissertation). Alliant International University, San Diego, CA.

Lovrien, K., Peterson, L. (2013). Strategically Positioning Health Systems in a Dynamic Environment. *Becker's Hospital Review.* Retrieved from . https://www.beckershospitalreview.com/strategic-planning/strategically-positioning-health-systems-in-a-dynamic-environment.html

Luke, C. H., Walston, E., & Plummer, M. R. (2004). *Strategic planning in hospitals.* San Francisco, CA: Jossey-Bass.

Maiga, A., & Jacobs, F.(2009). Leadership, nonfinancial, and financial Outcomes: The case of community hospitals. *Accounting and the Public Interest, 9,* 166-190.

McDonagh, K. J., (2006). Hospital governing boards. A study of their effectiveness in relation to organizational performance. *Journal of Healthcare Management,* 51(3).

McLaughlin, D. B., Militello, J., (2015). Thinking Beyond the Affordable Care Act. *Journal of Healthcare Management*, 60(3), pg. 161

McKinney, (2013). Medicare payments cut for more than 1,400 hospitals under value-based plan. *Modern Healthcare*, 43(46), pg.2

Meyer, H., Dickson, V., (2017). 24 million would lose coverage under GOP's Obamacare repeal plan. *Modern Healthcare*, 56(23), pg 9

Minkoff, D., Powell, W., (2006). *Nonprofit mission: Constancy, Responsiveness or deflection in the nonprofit sector.* New Haven: Yale University Press

Montoya, R.E. (2011). *An evaluation of the effects of the Baldrige criteria on hospital performance* (Unpublished master's thesis). California State University, Dominguez Hills.

Morrison, I. (2017). *Futurescan 2017 – 2022: Healthcare Trends and Implications. The Society for Healthcare Strategy & Market Development.* Chicago, IL: Health Administration Press

Muglia, V. O. (2010). *Relationship between environmental turbulence, Management support, organizational collaboration, information technology solution realization and process performance in healthcare organizations* (Unpublished doctoral dissertation). Alliant International University, San Diego, CA.

Nguyen, O. K., Halm, E. A., Makam, A. N. (2016). Relationship Between Hospital Financial Performance and Publicly Reported Outcomes. *Journal of Hospital Medicine*, 11 (7), pp. 481-8.

No author. *National Health Expenditure Fact Sheet 2015.* https://www.cms.gov/research-statistics-data-and-systems/ statistics-trends-and-reports/nationalhealthexpenddata/ nhe-fact-sheet.html

No author. *National Health Expenditure Fact Sheet 2017.* https://www.cms.gov/research-statistics-data-and-systems/ statistics-trends-and-reports/nationalhealthexpenddata/ nhe-fact-sheet.html

Noles, M. J., Reiter, K. L., Bootz-Marx, J., Pink, G. (2015). Rural Hospital Mergers and Acquisitions: Which Hospitals are Being Acquired and How are They Performing Afterwards? *Journal of Healthcare management*, 60(6), 395-408

Nguyen, O. K., Halm, E. A., Makam, A. N., (2016). Relationship Between Hospital Financial Performance and Publicly Reported Outcomes. *Journal of Hospital Medicine*, Vol 11 (7), pp. 481-488.

O'Brien, D. M., Kaluzny, A. D., Sheps, C. G. (2014). The Role of a Public-Private Partnership: Translating Science to Improve Cancer Care in the Community. *Journal of Healthcare Management*, 59(1), 17-29

Olden, P., & Smith, C. (2008). Hospitals, community health, and balanced Scorecards. *Academy of Health Care Management Journal, 4*(1), 39-56.

Ozmeral, A. B., Reiter, K. L., Holmes, G. M., Pink, G. H., (2012). A Comparative Study of Financial Data Sources for Critical Access Hospitals: Audited Financial Statements, the Medicare Cost Report And the Internal Revenue Service Form 990. *Journal of Rural Health*, Vol. 28 (4), pp. 416-24

Porter, M. E. (2010). What is the value in healthcare? *New England Journal of Medicine, 363*(26), 2477-2481.

Potter, S., (2001). A longitudinal analysis of the distinction between For-profit and not-for-profit hospitals in America. *Journal of Health and Social Behavior.* 42(1): pg. 17-44.

Porter, M. E., Pabo, E. A., & Lee, T. H. (2013). Redesigning primary care: A strategic vision to improve value by organizing around patients' Needs. *Health Affairs, 32*(3), 516-525.

Powers, T. L., Sanders, T. J., Stephens, M. E. (2013). Environmental and Organizational Influences on Magnet Hospital Recognition. *Journal of Healthcare Management,* 58(5), 353-366.

Rangarajan, A. (2016). Emerging Trends in Healthcare Adoption of Wireless Body Area Networks. Review: *Biomedical Instrumentation & Technology.* Allen Press Publishing Services

Ransom, S. B., Joshi, M. S., & Nash, D. B., (2005). *The healthcare quality book: Vision, strategy, and tools.* Chicago, IL: Health Administration Press.

Revere, L., Robinson, L., (2010). How Healthcare Organizations Use The Internet to Market Quality Achievements. *Journal of Healthcare Management* 55(1), 39-43.

Rice, S., McKinney, M., Evans, M. (2014, December 18). *More hospitals to get bonuses than penalties in 2015 under value-based purchasing.* Retrieved from Modernhealth care: www.modernhealthcare.com/artide/20141218/ NEWS/141219982/ more-hospitals-to-get-bonuses-than– penalties-in-2015-under-value

Richter, J. P., Muhlestein, D. B., Wilks, C. E. A., (2014). Social Media: How Hospitals Use It, and Opportunities for Future Use. *Journal of Healthcare Management* 59(6), 447-460

Robinson, P. D., (2016). Practitioner Application: Vision Statement Quality and Organizational Performance: *Journal of Healthcare Management*, 61(5)

Rodak, S. (2012). Hospital and Health System Strategy in 2012: 6 Key Initiatives. *Retrieved from Becker's Hospital Review*: www.beckers**hospital**review.com/**strategic**.../ **hospital**-and-health-system

Rubin, H.R., Pronovost, p., Diette, G.B. (2001). The Advantage and Disadvantages of Process-Based Measures of Health Care Quality. *International Journal of Quality in Health Care* 13: 469-7

Rundall, T., Oberlin, S., Salmon, K., Thygesen, B., Janus, K. (2012). Success Under Duress: Policies and Practices Managers View as Keys To Profitability in Five California Hospitals with Challenging Payer Mix. *Journal of Healthcare Management*, 57(2), pp. 94-111

Ruef, M., Mendel, P., & Scott, R. W. (1998). An organizational field approach to resource environments in healthcare. *Health Services Research Journal*, 32(6), 775.

Scott, W. R., Ruef, M., Mendel, P., Caronna, C. A., (2000). *Institutional Change and Healthcare Organizations*. Chicago, IL: University of Chicago Press Books.

Shactman, D., Altman, S. H., Eilat, E., Thorpe, K. E., Doonan, M., (2003). The Outlook for Hospital Spending. *Health Affairs*, Vol. 22

Shi, L., & Singh, D. A. (2008). *Delivering health care in America: A system approach.* Sudbury: Jones and Bartlett Publishers

Singh, S. R., Wheeler, J. (2012). Hospital Financial Management: What is The Link Between Revenue Cycle Management, Profitability, and Not-for-Profit Hospitals' Ability to Grow Equity? *Journal of Healthcare Management*, Vol 57 (5), pp. 325-39

Spath, P. (2009). *Introduction to Healthcare Quality Management*. Chicago, IL: Health Administration Press.

Swayne, L. E., Duncan, J. W., & Ginter, P. M. (2009). *Strategic management of health care organizations* (6th ed., pp. 3-33). Hoboken, NI: Wiley-Blackwell.

Taylor, N., Clay-Williams, R., Hogden, E., Braithwaite, J., Groene, O. (2015). High performing hospitals: A Qualitative Systematic Review Of Associated Factors and Practical Strategies for Improvement. *BMC Health Services Research.*

Totten, M. K. (2014). *Engaging Boards in the Transition from Volume to Value. Addressing the "why" before presenting the "how". Healthcare Executive,* 29(1), pp. 76-77

No author. Facts about Hospital Accreditation.Retrieved from . https://www.jointcommission.org/accreditation/accreditation main.aspx

Thomas, R.K., Calhoun, M. (2007). *Marketing Matters: A Guide for Healthcare Executives.* Chicago, IL: Health Administration Press.

Van Horn, R. L. (1997). *Environmental turbulence, organizational capabilities, and strategic response: Hospital strategy in an era of managed care* (Unpublished doctoral dissertation). University of Pennsylvania.

Whaley, C. M., Demirkan, S., Bai, G. (2023). What's Behind Losses at Large Nonprofit Health Systems? Health Affairs Forefront.

White, R. W., Griffith, J. R., (2010). *The Well-Managed Healthcare Organization.* Chicago, IL., Health Administration Press.

Wong-Hammond, L., Damon, L. (2013). Financing Strategic Plans for Not-for-profits. *Journal of the Healthcare Financial Management Association,* 67(10), pp.56-61

Zigmond, J. (2015). More Cuts Ahead. Obama's Budget Plan Opens Broader Deficit Debate. *Modern Healthcare*, 43(15), pg. 10.

Zuckerman, A. M. (2000). Creating a Vision for the Twenty-First Century Healthcare Organization. *Journal of Healthcare Management* 45(5).

Zuckerman, A. M. (2012). *Healthcare Strategic Planning*. Chicago, IL. Health Administration Press.

Zuckerman, A. M. (2014). Successful Strategic Planning for a Reformed Delivery System. *Journal of Healthcare Management*, 59(3)

APPENDICES

APPENDICES

APPENDIX A
NONPROFIT HOSPITAL SURVEY RESULTS

ID	Q1	Q2	Q3	Q4	Q5	Q6	Q7	Q8	Q9	Q10	Q11	Q12	Q13	Q14	Q15
1	Other, Nonprofit hospital	3	4	5	5	3	4	2	2	2	4	4	2	4	2
2	Nonprofit, local government hospital	3	2	3	3	3	4	3	4	4	5	5	4	4	2
3	Nonprofit, public community hospital	3	4	4	2	3	2	3	1	2	3	3	4	4	2
4	Nonprofit, public community hospital	1	3	4	4	4	3	4	2	2	5	5	4	4	3
5	Nonprofit, teaching hospital	4	3	4	3	4	2	2	4	2	5	4	4	4	3
6	Other, Nonprofit hospital	4	4	4	3	3	2	1	2	1	3	3	4	4	3
7	Nonprofit, public community hospital	3	4	3	2	4	4	2	3	2	4	3	2	4	3
8	Nonprofit, local government hospital	3	3	3	3	3	3	3	3	4	4	4	2	3	3
9	Nonprofit, local government hospital	3	2	2	3	2	3	2	2	2	2	3	2	3	2
10	Other, Nonprofit hospital	4	2	3	3	3	3	4	4	2	4	4	3	3	2
11	Nonprofit, state hospital	3	3	3	3	4	3	3	4	3	3	3	2	3	3
12	Nonprofit, public community hospital	5	4	4	4	2	1	1	1	2	2	1	1	2	1
13	Nonprofit, public community hospital	4	3	4	4	3	3	2	2	3	2	2	2	2	2
14	Nonprofit, local government hospital	3	3	3	3	4	3	4	5	4	5	4	4	4	3
15	Nonprofit, local government hospital	3	3	3	3	3	3	1	1	1	1	4	3	4	3
16	Nonprofit, state hospital	5	4	4	4	2	1	1	1	2	2	2	1	2	1
17	Nonprofit, local government hospital	3	3	4	3	2	1	1	1	1	2	2	1	1	1
18	Other, Nonprofit hospital	3	4	3	3	4	3	3	4	4	4	4	4	3	3
19	Nonprofit, teaching hospital	4	3	3	3	3	3	3	3	2	3	3	3	3	3
20	Nonprofit, local government hospital	3	4	3	2	3	2	2	4	4	3	4	4	4	3
21	Nonprofit, local government hospital	4	3	4	4	3	3	2	3	2	3	4	2	3	2
22	Nonprofit, local government hospital	4	4	4	4	3	3	1	1	1	2	3	2	2	2
23	Nonprofit, teaching hospital	3	3	3	3	3	3	3	3	2	4	4	3	3	3
24	Nonprofit, teaching hospital	3	3	3	3	3	4	3	4	3	3	4	4	4	3
25	Other, Nonprofit hospital	3	3	4	4	3	3	3	3	2	4	4	3	3	3
26	Other, Nonprofit hospital	1	4	2	2	5	4	4	4	3	4	5	4	4	3
27	Nonprofit, public community hospital	1	4	3	4	3	3	3	2	2	4	4	2	4	3
28	Nonprofit, local government hospital	4	4	4	4	3	3	2	2	4	3	3	3	3	3
29	Other, Nonprofit hospital	4	4	4	3	4	3	2	4	4	4	4	4	4	3
30	Nonprofit, local government hospital	4	3	3	3	3	3	2	3	3	4	3	4	3	3
31	Other, Nonprofit hospital	5	4	4	4	3	3	1	3	2	3	3	2	3	2
32	Nonprofit, teaching hospital	4	4	4	3	4	4	1	4	1	2	2	2	3	4
33	Nonprofit, local government hospital	3	3	3	3	4	3	3	3	4	4	4	3	3	3
34	Nonprofit, teaching hospital	3	3	3	3	4	4	3	4	2	2	3	3	3	3
35	Nonprofit, local government hospital	5	3	4	4	3	2	1	2	4	3	3	3	2	2
36	Other, Nonprofit hospital	3	3	3	2	4	4	4	3	4	4	4	4	4	3
37	Other, Nonprofit hospital	3	3	3	3	3	3	3	4	4	4	4	4	4	3
38	Other, Nonprofit hospital	4	4	2	2	4	4	4	5	5	5	5	5	5	4
39	Other, Nonprofit hospital	4	3	4	3	3	3	2	3	3	3	3	3	3	2
40	Nonprofit, local government hospital	1	4	2	2	5	5	4	5	5	5	5	5	5	5
41	Nonprofit, teaching hospital	4	3	4	3	4	4	2	3	2	3	3	2	4	3
42	Other, Nonprofit hospital	4	3	4	3	3	2	2	4	2	3	3	2	3	2
43	Nonprofit, local government hospital	4	2	3	3	3	3	3	3	3	3	3	3	3	3

APPENDIX A

Q16	Q17	Q18	Q19	Q20	Q21	Q22	Q23	Q24	Q25	Q26	Q27	Q28	Q29	Q30	Q31	Q32	Q33	Q34
4	4	5	2	5	1	2	4	3	4	4	4	1	1	0	0	0	0	0
4	5	2	2	4	1	2	4	4	4	4	4	1	5	0.02	3%	5%	0.09	3%
3	4	2	3	2	2	1	2	2	2	2	2	1	4	0.02	2%	0	0.012	4%
1	5	2	4	4	1	4	2	2	3	3	2	4	5	0.03	5%	6%	0.113	2%
5	5	3	4	3	2	3	3	2	3	4	3	5	3	0.5	1-2%	3%	0.06	4%
4	4	2	3	1	2	4	2	2	2	3	3	4	1	0.01	1%	2%	0.04	2%
3	4	2	4	2	2	2	3	4	4	3	3	5	4	0.04	4%	4%	0.05	4%
4	4	3	4	3	1	3	4	4	4	4	4	5	4	0.02253	2%	6%	0.043	4%
3	4	3	3	2	2	2	2	2	3	2	2	4	4	0.02	2%	1%	0.013	3%
4	4	3	3	3	1	3	3	3	4	4	3	5	4	0.04	4%	5%	0.04	4%
4	4	3	5	3	1	3	3	3	4	3	3	5	4	3.5	3.50%	7%	0.06	3%
3	3	2	1	2	2	2	2	2	2	2	2	1	1	0.01	1%	0.03	2.2298	-0.02
3	3	2	3	1	3	1	3	3	3	2	2	4	4	0.0071	0.71%	-0.0018	0.0033	0.13
4	5	4	5	4	1	4	4	4	4	4	3	5	5	0.12	12%	13%	0.2	0.14
4	4	3	4	3	1	3	4	4	4	4	4	5	5	0.0344	3.44%	0.14	0.16	0.05
2	3	2	4	2	2	2	2	2	2	3	2	4	3	-0.0109	'-1.09%	-0.0278	-0.0716	0.09
2	3	2	4	2	2	1	2	2	2	3	2	1	1	0.01	1%	0.04	0.07	0.01
4	4	4	5	3	3	4	4	4	4	4	4	4	4	0.02	2%	0.041	0.072	0.04
3	4	3	3	2	2	3	2	2	3	3	2	5	3	0.0132	1.32%	0.1071	0.102	0.026
4	4	3	4	2	1	4	3	3	4	3	3	5	4	0.005	0.50%	0.014	0.073	0.02
3	3	2	3	1	2	4	2	2	3	2	2	5	3	-0.0021	'-.2%	-0.01	-0.03	0.0046
3	3	2	4	2	2	3	2	2	2	2	2	4	2	-0.0006	0.06%	-0.00059	4.64	0.0004
4	4	2	4	3	2	4	3	3	4	3	3	5	3	0.026	2.60%	0.35	0.103	0.03
4	4	4	4	3	3	3	3	4	3	3	3	5	4	0.03	0.30%	0.04	0.09	0.04
4	4	3	3	3	2	4	3	3	4	3	3	5	3	0.0105	1.10%	0.06	0.102	0.015
4	5	4	4	3	4	4	4	4	4	3	3	5	4	0.055	5.50%	0.042	0.075	0.086
4	4	2	3	2	3	2	3	2	3	2	3	5	2	n	n	0.012	0.023	0.07
3	4	3	4	2	2	3	3	3	3	3	2	4	4	0.026	2.60%	0.075	0.105	0.044
4	4	4	4	2	3	3	3	4	4	3	3	5	4	0.0018	0.18%	0.009	0.0145	0.0184
3	4	3	4	3	3	3	3	3	4	3	3	5	4	0.0102	1%	0.05	0.0834	0.0193
3	4	2	3	2	3	3	3	2	3	3	2	5	3	-0.0242	'-2.42%	-0.073	-2.58%	-0.014
3	4	4	2	1	2	2	3	2	3	2	2	5	3	-0.0563	5.63%	-0.1323	-0.06	-0.04
4	4	3	2	2	3	3	3	3	4	3	3	4	4	0.03	3%	0.027	0.08	0.06
3	4	4	4	2	2	3	4	3	3	3	3	5	3	0.02	2%	0.036	0.054	0.04
3	3	2	3	2	3	3	3	2	2	3	2	5	4	-0.0069	'-.69%	-0.02	-0.024	0.02
4	4	4	4	3	3	3	4	4	4	4	3	5	5	0.06	6%	0.08	0.345	0.124
4	4	4	4	4	3	3	4	4	4	4	3	5	5	0.04	4%	0.1902	0.25	0.061
4	5	4	5	4	5	5	4	4	5	4	4	5	5	0.033	3.30%	0.103	0.165	0.053
3	4	3	3	2	3	2	3	3	3	3	2	5	3	-0.0011	'-.11%	-0.0028	-0.017	0.02
4	4	5	3	5	5	4	5	4	5	4	4	5	5	0.024	2.40%	0.052	0.088	0.051
3	4	3	3	2	2	3	4	4	4	4	3	5	3	0.0038	0.38%	0.035	0.118	0.008
3	4	3	4	2	2	4	3	2	3	2	2	5	3	0.009	0.90%	0.015	0.047	0.04
4	4	3	3	3	3	3	3	3	3	3	2	5	4	0.037	3.70%	0.166	0.116	0.067

APPENDIX A

APPENDIX B
NONPROFIT HOSPITAL TYPE
COMPLETING SURVEY

Nonprofit Hospital Type	Total Number of Hospitals
Other, Nonprofit Hospital	13
Nonprofit Local Government Hospital	15
Nonprofit Public Community Hospital	6
Nonprofit, State Hospital	2
Nonprofit, Teaching Hospital	7

www.ingramcontent.com/pod-product-compliance
Lightning Source LLC
Chambersburg PA
CBHW032053020426
42335CB00011B/314

* 9 7 8 1 9 6 3 0 5 0 2 6 4 *